# A SENSE OF PRIDE: The Story of Gay Games II

By Roy M. Coe

Principal Photography By Scott McLennan

Pride Publications / San Francisco, California

**A SENSE OF PRIDE:**
**The Story of Gay Games II**

**Author:**
Roy M. Coe

**Principal Photography:**
Scott McLennan

**Editors:**
Randall Weischedel, Kam Kammerer

**Book Design/Typography:**
Augustus Ginnochio/KeyStroke Productions

**Cover design:**
Kirk Frederick, Alton Wright
**Cover photo:**
Colston Young
**Photo editor:**
Scott McLennan

**Photographers:**
Thomas Michael Alleman, Joan Bobkoff, Cathy Cade, Rose de Castro, Shari Cohen, Daniel Collins, Roy Coe, Darlene, Jeanette Egger, Mick Hicks, David Hindley, John Jenner, Scott McLennan, Tony Plewik, Efren Ramirez, Steve Savage, Randall Weischedel, Colston Young

Copyright © 1986 by Roy M. Coe

All rights reserved. No part of this book may be reproduced or transmitted in any form or by any means, electronic or mechanical, including photocopying, recording or by any information storage from retrieval system without permission from the author, except for the inclusion of brief quotations in a review.

First Edition, 2,000 copies, December 1986

ISBN: 0-940681-00-5

\* \* \*

To order additional copies or
for information on reprints of photographs contact:
Pride Publications
2261 Market Street, Suite 306-B
San Francisco, CA 94114

(415) 552-3381

*This book is dedicated to Dr. Tom Waddell
whose vision and moral courage
sustained the Gay Games movement through the years,
and Shawn P. Kelly,
whose relentless energy and good humor
helped Gay Games II to realize its true potential.*

# ACKNOWLEDGEMENTS

I would like to thank the following individuals for their wonderful assistance, words of encouragement and moral support: Kirk Frederick, Shawn Kelly, Richard Baltzell, Richard Dopson, Kam Kammerer & Dan Russo, Tim Lewis, Doug DuFrene, Larry Holmes, Justin Cohen, Katherine Krebs and Ken Elyson.

I held over fifty interviews while working on this book, and my love goes out to all the athletes who shared their thoughts with me. I was proud to be with them at Gay Games II.

*Roy M. Coe*

---

It has been a long week of photography for this boy, yet the exhaustion I expect to feel is simply not there. What takes its place is a myriad of feelings, as I wander around the triangle outside Kezar Stadium, laughing and talking with athletes who in one short week have evolved from statistics to real people—flesh, blood and emotion.

I've seen the smiles, hugs, frustration, exhaustion and elation of 3,500 people who decided to "come out and play." Sharing this feeling of togetherness and acceptance has been one of the most uplifting moments of my life. This is the beginning, may the world take note.

As Tom Waddell said at the Closing Ceremonies, "We are not a minority, we're an *alternative*." Indeed. And how glorious it is to be a part of such shining individuals—to be able to share our love, our hopes and our dreams. Slowly, these qualities will replace the fear that has often crippled us.

We will no longer be slated as handicapped, as less than human. We have proven here that we are among the record breakers. We have taken adversity and crisis and responded to them with the strength of our achievements. AIDS and its fear have given us cause to take a deeper look at who we are and how we relate, and we are beginning to realize more of the beauty within. The Games are a tribute to that very diverse, very special beauty.

As some groups throughout the land pray to a vengeful god to have us destroyed, we serve notice that we are alive and healthy, and shall grow stronger in direct proportion to their fear of our existence. Through our love, through our self-acceptance, we are developing that strength.

Men, women, fathers, mothers, children—we are all of these. Let us continue to come out and play, to take hold of this wondrous life that pulses through us and experience the joy that is our birthright.

As Rita Mae Brown said at Opening Ceremonies, "Remember when you thought you were the only one?" May the Gay Games and this book that documents them help to transform the world so that our younger gay brothers and lesbian sisters will one day have no cause to live in fear and isolation. May we cherish our uniqueness and our love so that the world will have no choice but to realize the beauty within us *all*.

It has been a privilege to be with you at Gay Games II and to offer up these images that reflect the feelings we shared when we stood together and smiled one glorious smile. Let's keep it going, pushing through our fear and living in the love and freedom that only yesterday was a remote, far away dream. We are here, we are sublime and we are not going away.

Enjoy the book, live your life and express your love.

With love and respect,

*Scott McLennan*
August 17, 1986

# Contents

| | |
|---|---|
| Introduction | 6 |
| History of the Games | 9 |
| **Profile:** Dr. Tom Waddell | 12 |
| The Countdown | 18 |
| **Profile:** Shawn Kelly | 24 |
| Opening Ceremonies | 26 |
|     **Profile:** Sara Lewinstein | 32 |
|     **Profile:** Hal Herkenhoff | 33 |
|     Basketball | 34 |
|     Billiards | 37 |
|     Soccer | 39 |
|     Bowling | 40 |
|     Cycling | 42 |
|     Diving | 46 |
|     Triathlon | 50 |
|     Softball | 56 |
|     Physique | 60 |
|     Track & Field | 70 |
|     Marathon | 80 |
|     Powerlifting | 87 |
|     Volleyball | 90 |
|     Racquetball | 99 |
|     Swimming | 100 |
|     Tennis | 110 |
|     Wrestling | 113 |
|     Special Moments | 115 |
|     Procession of the Arts | 116 |
| Closing Ceremonies | 118 |

The Story of Gay Games II

# ☐ Introduction

The Olympic games in ancient Greece were celebrated every four years for nearly twelve centuries. The Olympiad marked a time for warring kings to lay down their arms and begin training their finest men for the prestige of representing their city.

Athletes were judged on two factors: the results of the competition and the grace with which the event was performed. Often, the first to cross the finish line was not declared the champion—a far cry from the electronic timing and elaborate scoring systems that characterize our modern day Olympics.

Imagine a foot race where every competitor is judged, as in competitive diving, on beauty, rhythm and style! This subtlety has been lost in the world of modern sports. We are conditioned to believe that winners take home the greatest prize. Defeating one's rivals is the ideal we are taught from a very early age.

*Wide World of Sports* neatly sums up our concept of competition: "The thrill of victory, and the agony of defeat."

So, too, have modern day politics served to subvert the unifying concept of the original Olympics. Jimmy Carter's boycott of the 1980 Olympics in Moscow is a recent example, along with the annual controversy over South Africa's participation in the Commonwealth Games. Governments have allowed their political agendas to cast a long shadow over the playing field, with their athletes as pawns upon it.

From the beginning, the goal of the Gay Games was to reverse this thinking. As Tom Waddell phrases it: "The message of these games goes beyond validating our culture. They were conceived as a new idea in the meaning of sport based upon inclusion rather than exclusion."

Translated into practice, this means that *all* people, regardless of sex, age, ability or nationality, are welcome to participate.

This policy is the foundation of San Francisco Arts and Athletics, the organization responsible for staging the events. From volunteers who stamped envelopes in the office, to Precision Dancers at the Opening Ceremony, individuals from all walks of life are welcomed to join in the celebration.

One story of Gay Games II that underscores this concept of inclusion involves the family of Kathy and Peter Lee. Kathy competed for Los Angeles in both basketball and racquetball; Peter played volleyball on a team from Washington, DC. Cheering them on from the sidelines were their mother and two sisters, who came with their families. At one of Peter's matches, their mother exclaimed, "Seeing all these attractive young men here makes me wish I was about thirty years younger . . . and I guess male."

And their father, in a wonderful gesture of love and support, entered the Gay Games swimming events. Peter and Kathy cheered on their Dad as he won the Lee family's only gold medal!

"For all of us," Peter says with obvious emotion, "the Games helped to take 'gay' out of the theoretical. The whole family was able to see a living example of gay people in harmony. Their involvement went beyond *toleration* to a positive statement of *affirmation* as well."

Most of the sports in Gay Games II were structured to allow athletes to compete against people their own age. Track and field, along with swimming, were officially sanctioned events in their respective national Masters programs, open to all athletes over the age of eighteen. Peter's father competes regularly in Masters swim meets, as do many of the athletes who came to San Francisco.

Above all stood the principle of *no minimum standards*. Men and women were encouraged to compete even if their interest was purely recreational. "We are all winners" became the message to this wide audience, including many who had never in their whole lives been sports-minded.

Our promotional brochure was titled simply: "COME PLAY".

In the Athletes Oath, given at Opening Ceremonies, the participants promised that all other athletes, whatever their standing, would be given support and encouragement. Indeed, some of the most inspiring moments in the Games came when senior gays enjoyed the cheers of support which have been denied to them for so many years.

I have been asked many times why gay people need to hold their own athletic events. Why not be satisfied with participation in the established sporting community?

This question raises many issues. The first, in my view, is that of visibility. The gathering of 3500 athletes at Gay Games II was an important demonstration of our love for each other and our presence in the world community. Our statement as a minority group was clearly made through the wonderful spirit of comaraderie and friendly competition.

As Armistead Maupin succinctly put it in his address at Closing Ceremonies: "The operative word here is gay, not olympics. The operative purpose is honesty, not athleticism."

Gay Games II was covered extensively in the media. We were surprised when CBS News showed up at our doorstep and ran a story on the Games for "The Evening News with Dan Rather." Their coverage, though slanted towards AIDS in the gay community, was an important step towards wider recognition of our right of self-expression.

Another issue is our support for diversity within the gay community. The inclusion of non-traditional events, such as bowling, golf and softball, was designed to attract those who compete in organized sports that are often more social than competitive in nature.

Our *Procession of the Arts*, which included over twenty-two cultural events, encouraged those with artistic interests who may have had no interest in sports whatsoever.

Further, the goal of health and well-being was repeated many times during the Gay Games. This was designed to stress our *spiritual* growth as well as physical.

Scott McLennan, whose photographs you will enjoy throughout this book, writes: "By giving the world a positive image of our unity and strength, we will have a great effect on how we are viewed by the world, and how we view ourselves."

None of these goals—inclusion vs. winning, support for alternatives, a sense of community and spiritual growth—can be achieved by hiding our differences and looking for support within the homophobic sporting community.

How many men and women ever feel the thrill of marching into a stadium to the cheers of thousands? Only the very best athletes make it to the regular "Olympics." Yet any athlete who had the courage to participate was welcome at Gay Games II, whose emotional content, witnessed by thousands in attendance, was unbelievably rich and powerful.

Throughout my travels in the U.S. and abroad, I have been impressed by the diverse motivations of gay athletes. Some competed in school and found sports to be a natural expression carried over from their earlier years. Some had taken up exercise during the fitness craze of the 70's, and still others sought gay athletics as a place to socialize in a non-threatening atmosphere.

Eric Caplan, interviewed in Atlanta but unable to attend the Games, commented:

"Most people in this area are going to be looking at this from the recreational side of sport, rather than from the competitive. Comaraderie has become very important for all of us because people are hungry for alternatives, looking for more stable friendships with gay people. Certainly sports represents a major avenue for doing just that."

This observation has helped me focus my attention on the unique nature of gay athletics. It brought a sense of fulfillment to my own interest in the Games and my goal of bringing them to life through this book.

Simply stated, athletics in the gay community offer hope, spirit and comaraderie to all who participate. And all are welcome. The Gay Games, and countless other organized events in our community, help to blur the distinction between competitive and recreational sport. This is no small achievement!

For two years I watched the excitement and anticipation of Gay Games II as it grew steadily towards August 9, 1986. I am proud to have shared in the collective vision and love that made these events possible.

This spirited week represents the culmination of my own desire for community involvement and a more positive self-image. I have met hundreds of athletes with similar dreams. Their lives, and the steady progress of history that brought them together, is the subject of this book. □

MICK HICKS

# History of the Games

## Gay Games I

The idea for a "gay Olympics" was first suggested at a Cable Car Awards ceremony in 1980 by Dr. Tom Waddell. There seemed to be widespread support for the idea. Tom joined forces with Mark Brown, and together they began to piece together the organization known as San Francisco Arts and Athletics (SFAA).

Many sports were already well organized. National leagues had been formed in tennis, softball and bowling. Key individuals from each of these groups were recruited to handle the logistics of staging the first Games.

The first entries to Gay Games I were received in early 1982. To facilitate participation, entries were accepted right up until Opening Ceremonies. The sporting and cultural events were held in late August of that year.

The first Games was marked by chaotic activity behind the scenes. The organizing committee and the administrative structure were built from scratch. There were no guidelines to draw from. No one had any experience in staging an event of this magnitude, and many key tasks were handled on an "ad hoc" basis.

Nonetheless, 1,300 athletes gathered in San Francisco to compete in sixteen sports. The Opening Ceremonies, planned and executed all in a matter of weeks, was highlighted by a performance by Tina Turner, just as she was hitting the comeback trail.

The week of sporting events was marked by warm feelings and spirited competition. After the Closing Ceremonies the verdict was nearly unanimous from volunteers, spectators and participants alike: Gay Games I had been an outstanding success.

The enthusiasm for organized sports was carried by athletes back to their hometowns like so many seeds on the wind. Soon, teams emerged in cities where sports activity had previously been lacking. National leagues were strengthened by a heightened awareness of gay athletics. Many of the athletes from 1982 returned to San Francisco four years later.

This ripple effect was overshadowed by the controversy that threatened to halt Gay Games I. Early on, it had been decided to use the name "Gay Olympic Games," and this brought down the wrath of the U.S. Olympic Committee.

*Oliver Murphy is congratulated by Doug Kimball following his gold medal in the Gay Games I decathlon.*

## Olympics Court Case

In 1978 Congress passed the Amateur Sports Act which, among other things, granted the United States Olympic Committee (USOC) exclusive use of the word "olympic." The USOC sought this favored treatment from Congress since it was impossible to seek trademark protection for a word that had been around for centuries.

In the summer of 1981, Dr. Tom Waddell was elected chairman of SFAA. Tom's background with the Olympics stretched back to 1968 when, as a captain in the U.S. Army, he competed in the decathlon event in Mexico City (see Tom's Profile).

As head of SFAA, Tom Waddell wrote to the USOC explaining that SFAA's use of the word "olympic" supported the goals of amateur athletics. In reply, F. Don Miller, the USOC's Executive Director and Tom's old rival from his army days, demanded that SFAA stop using the word, and threatened to "recover any and all funds which are solicited and acquired by virtue of the usage of 'Olympic' terminology."

The sparring began. After huddling with attorneys, including Mary Dunlap, SFAA vowed to continue using "Olympics" in its literature. Waddell wrote to Miller:

"We have been advised by legal counsel that there appears to be a violation of the guarantee of equal protection under the law .... There is a discriminatory action on the part of the U.S. Olympic Committee which has sanctioned the 'Junior Olympics' and 'Special Olympics,' but has looked the other way regarding the 'Armenian Olympics,' 'Xerox Olympics,' 'Crab Cooking Olympics,' 'Diaper Olympics,' 'Rat Olympics,' and 'Dog Olympics,' while at the same time takes exception to the term 'Gay Olympic Games.'"

The argument that the USOC was discriminating against gays was, however, a moot point. From a legal standpoint it made no difference that other violations of the olympic "trademark" had gone unpunished.

In a surprise action, the USOC responded by filing a court action on August 9, 1982, just two weeks before the Gay Games were scheduled to begin. A temporary restraining order was issued to prohibit the use of the word "olympic" in any form or context.

With just days remaining before athletes were due to arrive, SFAA was forced to eliminate the word from all souvenir items (T-shirts, posters, pins) and written materials. This effort alone cost an estimated $15,000. It also attracted national media attention.

*Sports Illustrated* ran an article quoting the International Olympic Committee Director, Monique Berlioux: "The U.S. Congress has no right to give away something that belongs to the IOC, least of all the Olympic emblem, which Baron Coubertin, the founder of the modern games, bestowed on the IOC and nobody else."

The article went on to say that the IOC complaint "makes it slightly awkward for the USOC to be screaming 'fowl' about the 'Gay Olympics.'" (*SI*, August 16, 1982)

Almost two years later, the USOC continued its legal harassment of the Gay Games. Represented in San Francisco by the high-powered firm of Pillsbury, Madison & Sutro, they filed suit in May of 1984 to recover legal fees of $96,600.

Federal Judge John Vukasin ruled in favor of the USOC to allow this financial judgment. SFAA attorney Dunlap was not allowed an oral hearing. Later the case took on a distinctly political tone when USOC lawyers attached a lien to the personal home of Tom Waddell, who was named as co-defendant.

SFAA appealed their case to the ninth district U.S. Court of Appeals in San Francisco. Their fiery attorney, Mary Dunlap, had defended many cases involving gay rights over the years. "This is an exceptional case," she began, as the first oral arguments were presented. It was a voice laden with urgency. The three judges of the court leaned forward in anticipation. Mary spoke angrily and with obvious emotional investment. She pounded on the issues of free speech and discrimination.

The courtoom was packed with gay and lesbian supporters. It was an intimidating setting with the federal judges seated in the front behind ornate oak partitions. The floor and walls were marble, the furniture a traditional heavy oak design. Benches for spectators were set in two rows in the back of the courtroom.

The opposing lawyers faced each other behind oak tables. Each side was

*Mary Dunlap, attorney for the Gay Games, who donates all her services pro bono.*

MICK HICKS

EFREN RAMIREZ

allowed thirty minutes to present their arguments at the lectern, facing the judges.

Mary's remarks were aired with force and conviction. The judges asked few questions, and listened intently. By contrast, the the USOC lawyers seemed jangled. They were interrupted regularly by the judges.

The arguments were over quickly and the long period of waiting for the decision began. Finally, in February of 1986, the Appeals Court handed down its decision: The word "Olympic" could not be revived for Gay Games II. The judges reaffirmed the USOC's right to police its trademark. They also remanded the issue of legal fees to a lower court for review, calling them "excessive."

In response, Mary Dunlap asked the Appeals Court to hear the case "en banc," that is, with all judges. The net result remained the same, but a strong dissenting voice emerged which offered hope. Alex Kozinski, a conservative judge appointed by President Reagan, wrote in his minority opinion that the issue "threatens a potentially serious and widespread infringement of personal liberties.

"If Congress has the power to grant a crown monopoly on the word 'Olympic,' one wonders how many other words or concepts can be similarly enclosed.... It seems that the USOC is using its control over the term 'Olympic' to promote the very image of homosexuals that SFAA seeks to combat."

Tom Waddell could not have said it more eloquently. Yet, in truth, the dissenting opinion carried no weight. The lien on Tom's house was still in place and the organization was still liable for $96,600 in legal fees.

Soon after the close of Gay Games II, papers were filed for an appeal to the Supreme Court. On October 20, 1986, the Supreme Court agreed to review the appeal.

### HISTORY
*Continued on page 14*

*(Opposite above) A marathon runner in Golden Gate Park. (Opposite below) The 4 x 200 mixed relay, with two men and two women per team, an innovation of Gay Games I.*

*(Above) The Board of Directors for Gay Games I on stage with Rita Mae Brown and Armistead Maupin at right.*
*(Right) Tina Turner dazzles the crowd at the Opening Ceremonies.*

**The Story of Gay Games II**

## Profiles

*"We have culture. We have a bona fide culture. It exists because the dominant elements in our society have told us that we're different, so we have been exploiting our differences."*

# Dr. Tom Waddell

### PRESIDENT OF THE BOARD OF DIRECTORS—
### SAN FRANCISCO ARTS & ATHLETICS □

Controversy, it seems, has followed Tom Waddell throughout his entire life. "I have never lacked for convictions," he states with insight.

This combative nature has brought with it its share of trouble. Yet along with controversy has also come the deep respect of the community. In 1980 Tom was honored at the San Francisco Cable Car Awards as "Outstanding Athlete," the same night he proposed the idea for an international gay athletic event.

Tom is a man, above all, who does not stray from his principles for the sake of expediency. Once he sets his sights, he is a tough man to deter. His quest to compete in the 1968 Mexico City Olympics is a prime example.

*Tom Waddell, with daughter Jessica, is greeted by SF Supervisor Louise Renne.*

The story begins when Tom was drafted into the Army but refused to be sent to Vietnam. He was a formidable adversary, well-spoken and intelligent. Tom's superiors were uneasy over arguing about the morality of war with a physician, and he was finally transferred to Walter Reed Medical Center in Washington, DC.

Tom had been very athletic in school, competing in gymnastics and track. He "always liked versatility." The intervening years of medical school and internship, though, had dulled his competitive edge. But seated behind his desk at Walter Reed, Tom read about Bill Toomey and dreamed about competing once again in the decathlon. As the 1968 Olympics approached, Tom petitioned the Army for a transfer to Fort MacArthur in Los Angeles, where Olympic hopefuls were training.

There he met many fine world-class athletes who helped to coach the "Old Man" in the ten events of the decathlon. At age 30, he won a place on the United States Olympic Team. Given his past involvement in the civil rights movement, Tom also joined forces with the "Black Caucus."

"We all made a pact," Tom recalls, "that if any of us won a medal, we would raise our hands in the Black Power salute in protest of racism, not only in the United States, but in the entire Olympic movement."

The black athletes who raised their clenched fists were immediately kicked out of the Olympic village. In an interview with the *New York Times*, Tom Waddell was quoted as saying, "There is visible evidence of USOC prejudice against black athletes." Army colonel F. Don Miller threatened Tom with a court-martial. (Miller went on to become the Executive Director of the U. S. Olympic Committee.)

Tom finished sixth in the decathlon, which he cites as one of the two proudest moments of his life. The other was the birth of his daughter Jessica, the child he co-parented with Sara Lewinstein.

Sara describes Tom as "self-motivated. He is one of those rare individuals you'll find who is very dedicated to whatever they get involved with. It he says he's going to become involved in something, he tries to put all of himself into it.

"The only problem is that he should say 'No' more often. He knows he can do something, and knows he can do it well, but he sometimes gets overextended."

The decathlon itself, based on the premise that you must excel in *all* events, is an appropriate metaphor for the life of Tom Waddell. Charismatic and persuasive, he has provided spiritual leadership for six full years to the Gay Games movement.

Throughout, he wanted to be involved in all facets of the Games—in essence, to play every sport. Yet many compromises were needed in order to stage this huge sports festival. And compromise is hard for a man with such strong beliefs.

A full range of committees emerged to handle the logistics of Gay Games II. Strong leaders in their own right carved out areas of responsibility such as Ceremonies and the Cultural Program. This was a far cry from Gay Games I, where Tom and many others filled in wherever needed. The new structure left Tom shy of direct participation in many decisions. As the founder of the

Gay Games watched his creation mature, one could sense his hesitation in letting go. But by 1986, the Gay Games had come of age.

In working with Tom Waddell, I was challenged time and time again with the power of his convictions. When the South Africa issue threatened to boil over, I cringed at the prospects of a boycott. Tom told me: "I have very mixed emotions over this issue. On the one hand it would be bad publicity if a South African team entered and the press got hold of it. But I am almost hoping that they do come so we can show the world our contempt for nationalism and our compassion for our gay brothers and sisters. The critical factor is that people represent *themselves* in the Gay Games, not a geopolitical entity."

The famous "olympic" court case, which has dragged on since 1982, stirs up an equally defiant posture. "Let's say we go to the Supreme Court and they say we can use the term in conjunction with the word "gay." I would start a campaign to say, 'We don't want it. It doesn't suit us anymore. It's tarnished.'

"We were using it initially to describe our Games, but let's look at the Olympics. The Olympics are racist, the Olympics are exclusive, they're nationalistic, they pit one group of people against another, and only for the very best athletes. That doesn't describe our Games."

Tom Waddell and his lover Charles once agreed to an interview with *People* magazine. The year was 1976, and a gay couple came out of the closet to a national audience. It was a significant step for the gay liberation movement.

While acknowledging progress, Tom feels that the community fails understand that this is a process that must be exploited. "More needs to happen," he argues. "Let's open *more* doors. Let's look at racism, ageism and sexism. But a lot of people see their sexual liberation as an end in and of itself."

Tom's goals for Gay Games II were solicited in our interview held two days before Opening Ceremonies:

"I want the community to see what terrific self-esteem and self-worth they should have. This starts at home ... I think gay people need to see it first. We need to know about ourselves.

"And the Games are just a format for this. Winning's not important, doing your best is important. These themes run over and over again. That's radical, revolutionary and recreational, as opposed to the sports page. I don't give a damn for reading about the salaries and the drug habits of professional athletes.

"*This* is sport. *This* is recreational. Here are the beautiful human interest stories. Ultimately, we have a lot to teach—about relationships and community support. And it all translates into an activity like the Games.

"We have culture. We have a bona fide culture. It exists because the dominant elements in our society have told us that we're different, so we have been *exploiting* our differences.

"We *are* different. We're wonderful! And we're worth knowing." □

---

*Just four weeks before the start of Gay Games II, Tom Waddell was diagnosed with pneumocystis carinii pneumonia. Yet with characteristic strength, Tom saw Gay Games II through to completion with pride and dignity. He competed in Track & Field and hurled a javelin 104 feet to win a gold medal. Most important of all, he was a spiritual leader for thousands of athletes who joined together to share in his dream.*

*At Closing Ceremonies, the Board of Directors gave Tom a plaque honoring him as "Papa Games." His inspiring remarks on this occasion can be found near the end of this book.*

Tom awards a gold medal in wrestling to Don Jung of San Francisco at Gay Games I.

The Story of Gay Games II

## HISTORY
*Continued from page 11*

## Preparations for Gay Games II

San Francisco Arts & Athletics (SFAA) is incorporated as a nonprofit organization. Following the first Games in 1982, an ad hoc committee continued to meet regularly. Their purpose was to determine if sufficient interest could by generated to stage a second Games in four years.

In the fall of 1984 I walked into SFAA's dusty office located in the Pride Center, a former convent which had been converted by the city into offices for gay community groups. On weekends the voices of the Gay Men's Chorus could often be heard drifting eerily through the hallways.

Most days, a man named Shawn Kelly held down the fort (see Shawn's profile). When we met, he was working as interim Executive Director, the post he later held on a permanent basis through September of 1986.

The Pride Center was an awkward place to do business, located as it was in a fringe neighborhood across from city housing projects. It left you with a strange, unsettled feeling and you often needed a sweater to fight off the chill. But day in and day out Shawn seemed to keep the Games alive through sheer force of will. Every letter received a personal reply, each caller was greeted with great enthusiasm.

In the spring of 1985, SFAA secured office space on the second floor of a building in the heart of the gay district at 526 Castro Street. The new quarters were warm, spacious and carpeted. The Pride Center was soon a distant memory.

The move helped to mark a spiritual change as well. By this time potential donors, volunteers and athletes began to believe that Gay Games II would really happen. Fund raising in particular had been difficult all along because the Games were so distant.

SFAA had been helped through lean months by steady supporters, notably Jack Campbell, a prominent financial backer. Still, we were often asked, "How can you expect me to give money for the Gay Games, two years away, when so much help is needed for AIDS *now?*"

The immediacy of the medical crisis, in fact, cast a shadow everywhere. Tom Waddell's philosophy was that "the Gay Games are not *about* AIDS. They are about health."

Shawn Kelly commented, "The Gay Games is the antithesis of the AIDS crisis. In many respects our community needs a psychological boost, and this will provide it. We are going to take this issue of AIDS and blast right through it."

The news media, as could be expected, focused on AIDS obsessively. It was difficult for us to promote healthy images of gay people when headlines of crisis dominated the front page of every newspaper.

San Francisco hosts a wide range of AIDS support groups, including the Shanti Project, SF AIDS Foundation, Coming Home Hospice and STOP AIDS, to name a few. The philanthropic support of the gay community had been growing to meet these important needs. It was hard to tap emotional support for the Gay Games when friends and loved ones were dying.

The Gay Games made a conscious effort to cooperate with these organizations through distribution of literature, joint fund-raisers and complimentary tickets for persons with AIDS. Following the Games, extra programs and posters were widely distributed without charge.

Persons with AIDS were encouraged to participate in sports, on committees, and in Opening and Closing Ceremonies as placard carriers, monitors and performers. Several joined the Golden Gate Precision Dancers, a group assembled just for the Games.

Christian Haren, a man who had been diagnosed with AIDS in the fall of 1983, used Gay Games II as a vehicle to rebuild his confidence and self image.

He competed in physique (also known as body building), an intense sport that requires long hours at the gym, a strict diet and a daily regimen of exercise. For a person with AIDS, this effort was all the more extraordinary.

Christian took the courageous step of contacting the media to publicize his efforts. He held interviews with local TV stations, *Time* and *Newsweek*.

Don Jung, a man well known in San Francisco for organizing the local gay wrestling club, had also been diagnosed with AIDS and still competed. Two days after winning a silver medal, he passed away.

The courage of these men and countless others was a reminder that the

---

*(Below) Christian Haren, a Person With AIDS, trains at a local gym and gets some moral support from a friend.*

THOMAS MICHAEL ALLEMAN

Games could offer tremendous hope and strength to the entire community.

## The Organization Takes Shape

Early on, Shawn Kelly structured his organization to be a loose federation of committees. Each month we met to review our progress and pass along information. It was often a surprise to hear about the hundreds of activities that were in motion elsewhere in the organization.

Sara Lewinstein and Hal Herkenhoff, Co-Directors for Sports, had also instituted regularly monthly meetings to review ongoing issues and progress.

The Board of Directors, meanwhile, addressed a number of key issues. The first was the concept of "parity." This SFAA policy meant that all public images representing the Gay Games should include both men and women, of all races, young and old.

From a public relations perspective, the execution of this concept was difficult. A dearth of photographs had survived Gay Games I and we constantly scrambled to find appropriate material.

One of the first advertising flyers included nine pictures donated by Mick Hicks, a local photographer who later served on the PR committee. Choosing the photos was an excruciating process, and everything was discussed carefully at the Board of Directors level.

The final result, despite all the confusion involved, was rich with life and

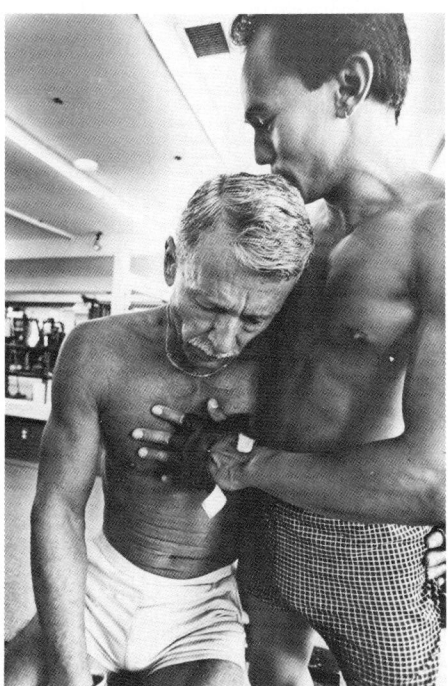
THOMAS MICHAEL ALLEMAN

*(Left) Alain Scofield, a local artist and head of Decorations, prepares the marathon start sign.*

energy. The caption read: *IN AUGUST 1986, SOMETHING WONDERFUL WILL HAPPEN... FOR THE SECOND TIME.*

The need for parity was important for another reason: to keep harmony between the men and the women in the organization. The solution at the Gay Games was to insure that responsibility was shared on committees wherever possible. Most sports, for example, were evenly handled by two chairpersons, one man and one woman.

Women on the Board of Directors, notably Sara Lewinstein, fought tooth and nail for this equality of representation. In retrospect, it would have been easy to slide into a male dominated organization, reflective of American sports in general.

Balance was made possible through the efforts of many respected women who served on the Board: Rikki Streicher (a guiding light), Jean Nelsen (finance), Rose Mary Mitchell (fund raising), Chris Puccinelli (business sponsorships), Mary Dunlap (attorney) and, of course, Sara Lewinstein herself (Co-Director of Sports).

Lloyd Jenkins, also on the Board, chaired the Outreach committee. One of his organization's several responsibilities was to support the concept of inclusion—for women, seniors, minorities, and the international community.

Board member Paul Mart, our roving and fun loving ambassador, promoted the Games for years on trips through Europe, the Far East and the "land down-under," all from out of his own pocket. Yet our communication with gay men and lesbians in other countries was difficult, and was always hindered by a limited budget.

Strong gay athletic groups exist in both Australia (Melbourne, Sydney) and Canada (Toronto, Vancouver). Other countries were harder to reach, even though gay communities thrive there. For example, the records show only one athlete entered from West Germany, and one from the Netherlands.

The size of each city's contingent depended upon the resourcefulness of local organizers. A large team of twenty-three was drawn from France due to the efforts of one man with a vision, Pascal Bibbolet, and the support of *Gai Pied*, a major gay paper in Paris.

In the spring of 1986 the Opening & Closing Ceremonies Committee, headed by Katherine Krebs, presented their proposed program to the Board of Directors. Surprisingly, the issue of national flags was debated at length: should athletes be allowed to carry them into Kezar Stadium?

One viewpoint, held by Tom Waddell, was that flags represented nationalism. The Gay Games goal, as set out in its charter, was to eliminate the need for national distinctions. The Games were open to all, regardless of political or social background. Nationalism was a disunifying concept, Tom argued. Athletes were invited to represent their city, not their country.

The counter-argument was based on practical and aesthetic considerations. It was hard to imagine Opening Ceremonies without the color and excitement of flags and banners in the athlete's procession. As one Board member put it, "You know they are going to bring their flags, regardless. What are you going to do, rip them out of their hands as they make their way into the stadium?"

The traditionalists won out, and flags were in.

## South Africa

The policy of including all people (and all countries) in the Gay Games brought the issue of South Africa into the forefront, not once but many times. 1986 was a year in which the policy of apartheid was the subject of hot debate throughout the world.

In late September 1985, SFAA received a letter from the International Gay Association asking "...if you are following the UN guidelines calling for the boycotting of South African athletes." At its annual conference the IGA had urged a boycott of the Gay Games unless assurances were given that these athletes would be excluded.

This was followed shortly by a letter from the Scottish Homosexual Rights Group, headed by Ian Christie, raising similar questions. The Board of Directors met in December and reaffirmed its stance that *all* athletes, regardless of country, were welcome. A position paper was drafted. It read, in part:

"We are being asked to exclude gay sisters and brothers from a country where such persons are already outlawed and oppressed. To restrict an individual from South Africa from participating in the Gay Games would create a double jeopardy for that individual, and would be against the purposes and goals of SFAA and the Gay Games."

The Scottish group continued its call for a boycott, catching the ear of *The Body Politic*, a gay paper in Toronto. That spring the item was picked up in the *Pink Triangle* published in New Zealand and *Campaign* in Australia.

It is hard for Americans to appreciate the political furor that apartheid has raised in the southern hemisphere. On my trip to New Zealand I passed through Christchurch on a Sunday afternoon. At the airport I was startled to find heavy security holding back crowds of people and TV news crews.

Once inside, I heard people chanting, "Shame! Shame! Shame!." Their target: athletes who were leaving for South Africa to play their national team in rugby.

Soon thereafter, Owen Shanks, a friend in Wellington, wrote me an urgent letter. He had been contacted by HART, a political group responsible for disrupting previous rugby matches in New Zealand. Their tactics included civil riots, smoke bombs and invasion of the rugby fields to spread nails, tacks and glass.

HART had been alerted by reports in the gay press, and they urged Owen to boycott the Games. In San Francisco, several anxious weeks passed as the athlete registration deadline approached. More letters of protest were received including one that promised a boycott and demonstration at Opening Ceremonies.

The June 1 deadline finally passed with no South African entries. From a PR viewpoint, it was a time of great relief. Apartheid had become a lose/lose proposition. The Games would suffer if we banned any athlete (regardless of the reason). Yet if an athlete from South Africa had entered, the media would have feasted on the negative publicity.

There was simply no way to win a political argument on the subject. Apartheid had emerged as the liberal litmus test of the eighties. The issue had no place in the Gay Games, whose stated goal was to disregard nationalism. But this larger agenda was forced on us because of outside circumstances.

As Owen Shanks summed it up: "Bloody politics and sport!"

## Homophobia

On occasion, our efforts to reach the gay community worldwide touched upon the raw nerve of homophobia. As a function of Outreach, we mailed Gay Games posters to several hundred businesses listed in *Bob Damron's Guide*. The following letter was received from a lawyer in Iowa:

"The owner of The Good Life Lounge consulted me with reference to a letter she received. We would ask that you refrain from sending any such materials regarding gay activities, in that this establishment does not support or encourage any of your activities or philosophies. The Good Life is not a gathering place for gay individuals, and if there is such a place here in Mason City, it certainly is not at The Good Life Lounge."

Or take the case of an athlete registered in Volleyball:

"I received information and other material from you concerning 'Gay

*(Left) The San Francisco swim team hosts a car wash fundraiser. Even out of the pool, there was plenty of water to go around.*

Games' [our preregistration packet]. I *highly object* to you sending me such media and also having my name and address designated as a participant. I don't know where you got my personal information but please do not consider me for your games any more. I am completely "Heterosexual."

Completely? He should talk to the team captain who submitted the roster!

And finally, this note from New York City:

"Please remove me immediately as representative of the GBL, Inc., or Gay Brotherhood Liaison. I have not been a member of that organization for several years now, and I cannot tell you who to address in my place.

I am anxious to point out to you that much of this country and the world does not espouse the libertine view of Castro Street! Your choice of the 'long spelling' [for G B L on our mailing label] only serves to indicate how provincial you are at a time when you are involved in an earnest promotional effort: the people at my home address have no knowledge of my way of life, preferences, etc.—or at least they *had no such knowledge* prior to your clumsiness!

"I advise you to remove my name immediately from your mailing lists and not to contact me ever again, or I shall be forced to institute legal action. I trust that I have made myself perfectly clear."

SFAA had made a conscious effort to package all its letters and publications discreetly, and most of our contacts were friendly and supportive. But these letters served to remind us that gay men and lesbians in other cities are far more careful, with good reason, than those of us in San Francisco. For better or for worse, it is possible here to have exclusively gay friends, work at a gay establishment and not deal with the prejudices of the outside world. There are few places in the world that offer such freedom. □

*(Left) A pre-Games squeeze as swimmers line up for their team picture (below).*

# ☐ COUNTDOWN

June 1, 1986, the athlete's entry deadline, was a milestone in the weeks leading up to Gay Games II. Entries had opened with little fanfare in March of 1985. By year end, 173 athletes had signed up. Many of these athletes entered the marathon, a sport which demands a long period of training. During the spring months of 1986, Hal Herkenhoff and Sara Lewinstein, Sports Directors, agonized over the slow pace of entries.

By early May the total count was 761 (about half of the total entries in Gay Games I). A week before the deadline, 1,462 had been received. As the days ticked off, a deluge of entries hit the Gay Games office. It was like an income tax deadline with everyone, waiting until the last possible minute.

Batches of Express Mail arrived daily. The postman, a lumbering man who had once (no doubt) enjoyed the pace of his job, staggered up the long stairs to our office a couple of dozen times. At first cheerful, he was dour and cranky by the end of this surge.

June 1st was a Sunday and we were open all weekend for walk-in entries. Athletes arrived in droves and the office at 526 Castro Street looked as though it were under siege. A last minute decision was made to allow all mail postmarked by Monday, June 2nd to be accepted. Many entries arrived after the cutoff, but Hal and Sara stood firm: no exceptions would be made.

The office crew began the task of entering all the names into our personal computer, nicknamed Maggie. But soon she bogged down and had to be replaced with a faster unit known as Rita.

A month later the dust had settled, and a tally of 3,482 athletes were entered in the seventeen sports of Gay Games II. The ratio of men to women was almost exactly 3:2. This represented an outstanding job of outreach to the women's community.

The sports committees had been planning their activities for months based only on estimated entries. Now each Sports chair had real numbers to go by, along with team rosters and breakdowns according to event.

We called a press conference on July 9th to announce the entries. The press turnout was light, as always, and we received only modest coverage in the local media. But *we* knew that our momentum alone would carry us through August.

Enthusiasm over the number of entries was heightened by a growing awareness of the event in the community. Our public relations efforts were beginning to take effect. My PR commitee was exuberant when the Board of Directors voted to double the advertising budget from $20,000 to $40,000. Around the same time, the city's Hotel Tax Fund granted the Games $30,000 towards promotional expenses.

Shawn Kelly's vision was to promote the Gay Games as a festival that would go beyond a typical gay event. To do this we focused on the mainstream media. Our first target was billboards placed in MUNI subway stations, from Castro Street to the Embarcadero downtown. Thousands of commuters were treated to a montage of athletes and the Gay Games logo. Later we ran messages on the overhead subway platform signs, including one that extolled our *FAAABULOUS CEREMONIES*.

Our most outrageous expenditure was a radio campaign on four mainstream stations in the San Francisco Bay area. The radio ads began with a short pitch by members of San Francisco's Board of Supervisors. All but one were eager to add their voice and name to our campaign. (Several were poised to run for mayor in the fall.) The text of the commercial was read by Don Bleu, a drive-time DJ and local legend. It was startling, but effective, to hear the words "Gay Games II" jump out of the radio!

The beginning of summer in San Francisco is marked by the Gay Pride Parade, held in late June. We worked hard to promote a major show of strength for this event. It was a perfect way to reach out to the gay community and remind

*(Opposite page) Pat Desch, a fun-loving volunteer, heads to the post office with registration kits. (Below) John Molinari, President of the SF Board of Supervisors, Shawn Kelly and Katherine Krebs at a pre-Games news conference.*

ROY COE

The Story of Gay Games II

them of the Games in August.

Parade day in 1986 was sunny and beautiful. Few could remember such a wonderful feeling from the crowd in recent years. The Gay Games marching contingent included athletes from each sport. The swimmers swam, the wrestlers wrestled and the body builders flexed

their way up Market Street to the plaza at City Hall. Our booth did a landslide business in T-shirts.

More importantly, dozens of volunteers signed up to help us in the weeks to come. Volunteers would provide the key to our success that summer. The challenge was to find them, keep their interest up and assign them jobs that would benefit the Games.

A phenomenal amount of logistical work was crammed into the six week period between the parade and Opening Ceremonies. These days were hectic and filled with last minute planning and coordination.

Shawn warned all his committee chairs: "Don't assume that someone else is handling it." The goal was to be sure that nothing would slip through the crack.

50,000 Official Programs were printed (80 pages each). Where would they be stored? The Registration Center. When would they be ready? Just in time. How would they be distributed? Just ten days before the event, we discovered that no one had been assigned to deliver 40,000 programs out to Kezar Stadium for Opening and Closing Ceremonies.

Athletes from the Bay Area would register on August 2nd and 3rd, a week before the Opening. Would badges be ready? They arrived in plenty of time, but not on continuous computer forms.

Could they be typed? Calls went out for a battery of typewriters.

Meanwhile, Barry Hochman, our computer wizard, figured out a way to print the forms on a PC printer. A week later, the badges were complete with each athlete's name and sport.

How fast were tickets selling? Slow but steady. It was a shock to learn, however, that BASS, the local ticket agency handling the event, would not reimburse us until *after* the Ceremonies. Quickly, advertising was shifted to play down BASS and steer ticket buyers to our office. Cash was needed to pay a steady stream of bills.

Hanging from the fire escape outside the office was a countdown sign with DAYS LEFT until the Opening. Shawn Kelly's comment during the final weeks: "I know that everything is OK when I change the sign in the morning, then climb back in the window with the satisfaction that I didn't jump off."

Shawn's humor and good nature during this time contributed to buoy the spirits of volunteers in the office. Moments after dealing with an angry patron or some similar emergency, he would unleash a quip which lightened the mood and brought a smile to your face.

Activity in the office was relentless. Between 8:00 and 9:00 each morning it was possible to concentrate. By 10, the phones would be jammed and a constant flow of foot traffic prevailed. One Friday, I looked up and counted nineteen volunteers in the office. Many were preparing athletes' registration kits. Others were staffing the phones, matching hosts with guests and selling tickets. It was a pretty amazing turnout for three in the afternoon.

Jan Allen, Co-Chair of Registration, was in the office constantly, tending to the infinite array of details relating to the athletes. Board members, notably Peter Middendorf, helped out at the Ticket Desk. The Ticket Hotline recording ran continuously once radio commercials started giving out the number.

Cindy, our Office Manager, could often be found keeping entries up to date on the computer. Her good nature and deadpan humor provided a constant reminder that we need not take ourselves too seriously.

The Sports committees also saw their pace of activity grow steadily as the days ticked away. Sports directors Hal and Sara put in steady hours to handle the last minute changes in roster and keep each sport committee on track for their event.

Derek Liecty, head of Facilities, handled all the details concerning contracts and access for the multiple venues. Derek's three-ring binder was legend at the office. It contained every piece of Facilities correspondence, along with contracts for all the sites where sporting events would be held. Given seventeen sports, staged on both sides of the Bay, this was no mean feat.

Among his many logistical duties were transportation and concessions. Obtaining permits with city agencies often bordered on the surreal. Derek, who remained cheerful throughout his volunteer tenure, termed a certain department "one of the more draconian bureaucracies I have encountered."

One of the largest challenges for Gay Games II involved the need for insurance of all kinds. Derek had finally secured $500,000 liability insurance through Schmidt and Schmidt, a local gay-owned agency. However, the city of San Francisco (owner of Kezar Stadium) required $1 million coverage. After a few days of frantic calls to various officials, we were granted a waiver on this requirement.

This was, at least, a hurdle that was anticipated in advance. The insurance caper that caught everyone off guard involved the headliner for Closing Ceremonies. Just as the contract negotiations reached their critical stage, Jennifer Holliday's agent asked for a $1 million dollar policy ... *on Jennifer herself!*

The search for a top entertainer had been a wild affair. The Program Committee, reporting to Katherine Krebs (Director of Ceremonies), had compiled a list months earlier, and a talent agent began to work on the top candidates.

We were tantalized by the prospect that Bette Midler would be signed. There had been hopeful signs and we could hardly contain ourselves. Fill the stadium? Nooooo problem.

But ultimately the curtain fell on the deal with Bette Midler, and the Program Committee was back to square one. Patti Labelle was approached, but her asking price was too high.

Finally, in late June, Katherine announced that Jennifer Holliday was close to signing. We began to pull together ad copy and a press release. 250 publicity shots of Jennifer were prepared. We agonized through contract negotiations, complicated by the insurance question.

The pitch of activity at 526 Castro Street could be measured by sound of the phones. Four lines were in constant use, in addition to the Ticket Hotline number (a pre-recorded message).

A growing concern following the June 1st entry deadline concerned out of town athletes who needed housing in private homes. The billeting situation in Gay Games I paled in comparison to the challenges in 1986.

Susan Quillin, Housing director, was masterful in attracting a team of volunteers to follow up with athlete requests on the one hand, and hosts on the other. It took patience to explain to anxious hosts that not everyone could house the Australian swimming team. Eventually, over *1200* men and women were tucked into spare beds, sofas and futons.

A month before the opening of the Games, I had the opportunity to visit Kezar Stadium with Bud Coffey, who would later direct the show from high up

*(Above) Volunteers Pat Desch, Susan Quillin, Jan Allen and Gary Bozzini ham it up during a lull in registration, while a mascot (left) stands guard.*

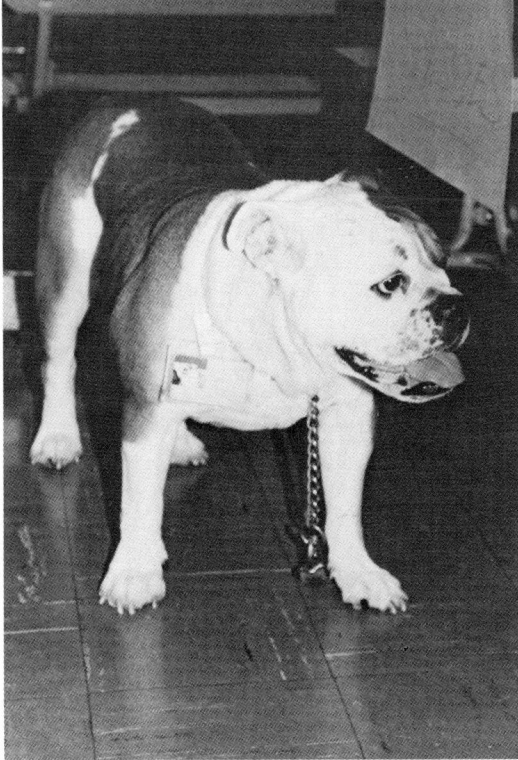

**The Story of Gay Games II**

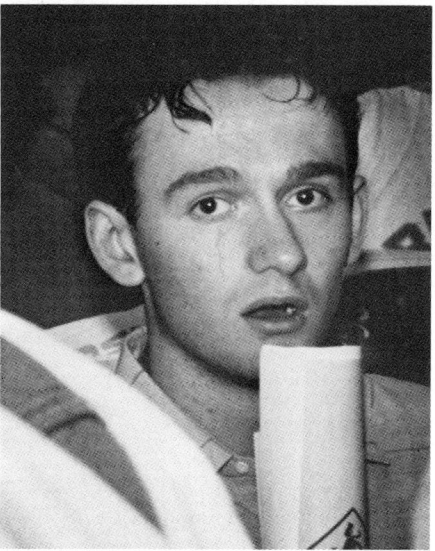

*(Above) Visitors pour over maps of San Francisco, while a French athlete (right) tries to figure out the next step in registration.*

*(Opposite page) Kezar Stadium stands ready for the Parade of Athletes and thousands of spectators at Opening Ceremony.*

in the press booth. We arrived in early afternoon and drove down to the west end of the field.

Kezar, once the home of the San Francisco 49ers, had been neglected for years. The wooden bench seats were peeling and weeds grew up through cracks in the cement. But the field itself was absolutely immaculate. The grass, cropped short, was beautifully kept. Eamon Bowler, the groundskeeper, had worked at Kezar for over twenty years. He remembered the warmth of Gay Games I and was pleased to see us return.

We climbed through the stands and up into the press booth, which offered a panoramic view of the stadium. To the east, Bud gestured to where the massive stage would be built. To the west stood the portal through which the athletes would parade onto the track.

As Bud spread out the blueprints, I looked up suddenly and felt a spine-tingling chill run up my back. Tears came to my eyes as I imagined the climax of our years of preparation. The stadium was a beautiful sight. It was hard to leave that afternoon and head back to the office.

By late July, dozens of committees were in the final stages of panic. *Procession of the Arts* events were ready to begin August 1st. The Golden Gate Precision Dancers rehearsed twice a week. Athlete's packets were mailed out, followed soon by registration. Finishing touches were applied to awards platforms, banners, flags and signs. Volunteers were recruited for key jobs at each sport venue. Last minute orders for tickets were taken by phone.

Volunteers pulled together in a wonderful spirit of cooperation, and the excitement peaked as athletes began to arrive. Colorful team uniforms appeared on the streets and foreign accents could be heard in restaurants.

Finally the day arrived that we had anticipated for so long: Saturday August 9, 1986, the day of Opening Ceremonies for Gay Games II. It was cold and foggy in San Francisco. Athletes in their warm-up suits lined up early at the Registration Center. I arrived at the Games office around 9:00 AM to pick up last minute supplies. I was surprised to find Shawn Kelly feverishly manning the phones, alone in the office, an hour before gates at Kezar Stadium would open.

We had worked together for nearly two years and a knowing glance passed between us. Quickly we changed the message tapes on both answering machines: "Tickets can be purchased at the gate . . . go to Kezar . . . go to Kezar."

We hugged, then locked up and headed towards the stadium. The phones kept ringing.

*"We are saying to the world: 'We are alive, we are well—and we are here to stay.'"*

# Shawn Kelly

EXECUTIVE DIRECTOR, GAY GAMES II □

SAN FRANCISCO, CALIFORNIA □

"Growing up, I was accustomed to believing in and doing things that were totally outside the mainstream, things that were considered to be hostile actions against the community. For me, though, they were always natural instincts, inclinations and beliefs."

Born in Anniston, Alabama, Shawn Kelly was raised by liberal parents in the deep South where necks were red and racism ran deep. "Word was out that we were different, that we lived by different standards than most other people in town."

A dichotomy emerged as he sought recognition from classmates in school ("I was always running for class president") yet found refuge in activities that gave him time alone, including tennis. This sport was an anomaly in a state where football reigns supreme.

He found college at Vanderbilt, in Nashville, Tennessee, 300 miles to the north, to be only slightly more enlightened ("I roomed next to an ardent fan of Lester Maddox"). From there he moved to Washington, DC and took a job working for Ralph Nader.

Six months of hard work helped foster Shawn's interest in public affairs. The job paid little but the visibility was high. He moved to San Francisco on Halloween, 1978.

"At that time," he recalls, "I wasn't just in the closet, I was still in the vault!" The Halloween celebration in San Francisco was a real shock to this Alabama boy.

"I went out to Polk Street and saw 6' 5" men in drag . . . and got right back in my car."

The city eventually worked its charm, and Shawn settled down as a reporter for the gay newspaper *The Sentinel*. Soon, he found his way into the Gay Tennis Federation (GTF), "the beginning of my life in any serious sense as I began to make real friends." Under Les Balmain's leadership, the GTF's membership grew rapidly, as did Shawn's involvement. It was a theme that played well into his love for public affairs.

"Gay culture is just now developing the elements that make it a community with institutions, large and small, institutions that have a history to them, that perform services for people, and that draw gays together around similar interests. The rapid rise of the GTF is a demonstration that it was just waiting for someone with the organizational abilities to create it."

The Gay Tennis Federation had already staged two national tournaments when Gay Games I rolled around in 1982. Shawn served as tennis tournament director. "The primary reason I got involved was that all these athletes had taken a step, a brave step, to parade in front of thousands of people and acknowledge that they were gay."

As the momentum for Gay Games II began to build, he found himself in the the right place at the right time. Gay athletics was a perfect combination of community service, high visibility and challenge, and a "vehicle for advancing the gay liberation movement."

Shawn first worked as a secretary for San Francisco Arts & Athletics (SFAA), then office manager, associate director, and finally executive director by December of 1984.

As SFAA's only paid employee, Shawn faced the task of recruiting volunteers to handle the logistics of Gay Games II. He crafted a committee structure and found men and women who would take the lead in such areas as registration, facilities, medical support and housing. Those who got involved shared many of Shawn's own qualities: the willingness to take risks, assume responsibility and work as a team player.

Group morale was boosted by Shawn's popular monthly staff meetings, all-morning affairs highlighted by croissants and lively discussion. They served to let the right hand of SFAA know what the left hand was doing. Did Housing need Advertising to attract more hosts? Did Sports need awards platforms built?

By the spring of 1986 Shawn was working six days a week. He compared the final months to "hitting the wall, a seemingly impenetrable barrier. When you push through that wall, you find this renewed level of energy and stamina that carry you through."

His steady relationship with his lover Ron helped maintain sanity outside of the office. "When we come home we're in the safety zone. We turn on the answering machine, shut off the world and try to have some private life and time to ourselves."

As the Games activity reached its peak in late July, Shawn showed his cool under fire. He was constantly in the public eye, yet managed to avoid alienating any major segment of the gay community. Asked what kept him going, Shawn replied simply, "Coffee!"

Under his leadership, San Francisco Arts and Athletics staged Gay Games II for thirty-five hundred athletes with a budget of $650,000. At the peak of activity in August 1986, over a thousand volunteers had been recruited to work on various committees and assist at the seventeen sports venues.

After the last athletes had left Kezar Stadium and headed home, the financial tally began. Invoices were balanced against ticket and souvenir sales. Shawn fended off creditors while the bookkeeping continued. Five weeks after Closing Ceremonies, he received the welcome news: Gay Games II could pay all its bills with room to spare. It was a great compliment to his executive abilies.

Shawn's warm sense of humor contributed greatly to his success. He had a knack for making a quip at the right time, and was generous in his praise, which kept motivation high. This applied to everyone, from a committee person faced with life and death decisions to a volunteer entering data on the computer.

"Look at us!" he exclaims. "The Games are available to people from all walks of life, all economic and racial backgrounds, and all political strides. That is one of the things that excites me about working here. Although we may view it in different terms, we have drawn all sorts of people in the community into a common effort.

"We are saying to the world: 'We are alive, we are well—and we are here to stay.'"

Shawn Kelly sought the limelight and survived the highest pressure in his position with Gay Games II. It reminds him of his Alabama roots, in a liberal family surrounded by prejudice. "My uncle pioneered the sport of tennis in that town," Shawn recalls. "He used to say, 'You're like a rabbit in a plowed field. You're out there on the court all alone, and everyone can see you, and it's all on your shoulders.' So you can understand why the Gay Games have been satisfying to me."  □

TONY PLEWIK

"I couldn't have hired better leaders—or found better friends." Shawn's volunteer crew: front row—Susan Quillin (Housing), Jan Allen (Registration), Katherine Krebs (Ceremonies), David McLaughlin (Registration); second row—Sue Barnett & Bill Woods (Volunteer Services), Cindy Grundman (Office), Derek Liecty (Facilities), Sara Lewinstein (Sports), Shawn Kelly; rear—Michael Clarke (Procession of the Arts), Dick Rosen (Planning), Hal Herkenhoff (Sports), Larry Holmes (Publications), Roy Coe (Communications), John Hoover (Graphics), Bud Coffey (Ceremonies); missing from photo - Alain Scofield (Decorations), B.J. Irwin (Security), Charlie Williamson, MD (Medical).

**The Story of Gay Games II**

*Welcome athletes! Is this the best party of the twentieth century or what? Now I want everyone who is single to raise their right hand. Okay, now did everyone get a good look? You've got one week!*
—Rita Mae Brown

# ☐ Opening Ceremonies
### AUGUST 9, 1986

The Story of Gay Games II

# Invocation

## Reverend Jane Spahr

Founder, Marin AIDS Network
Executive Director, Ministry of Light,
Marin County, California

Our Source, we are here to celebrate who we are as lesbian women and gay men. We are here with family, friends and loved ones who wish to celebrate with us the joy of being together to affirm who we are. You who are the source and giver of life, you who ask us to join you as co-creators, we ask your continued blessing as we enjoy and play in these many sports over this next week.

Our foremothers and forefathers did not have this kind of opportunity, and we thank you that here today we know and continue to seek the wholeness that gay and lesbian persons can and will enjoy. For you will grow with all of your world until all of us labeled "different" are free.

On this day our community feels a real sense of commitment and purpose to remember not only our joy, but to stand and be with our many gay brothers who are not here because of AIDS. We ask your comfort in their courage, your love in their healing, your care in their care.

There are no words to thank you enough for giving us the freedom to be here today from all the many countries across your world. Your love for us is immeasurably grand. We take, then, a moment of silence to thank you for loving us into being, and to remember those who have helped us to be here this day. Grant your world peace and unity, we pray—the peace you know, and the unity we imagine. □

ROSE DE CASTRO

# MC / Opening Ceremonies

## Rita Mae Brown

It's wonderful to be back with my brothers and sisters four years later, and the Games are continuing. I would like to welcome all of you on behalf of the organizers, the athletes themselves, the officials, and all of the people who made possible this incredible event that we have come to know as the Gay Games.

And I emphasize "gay" in Gay Games. These Games are very important to us, not just because they bring us all together, but because here we show the world who we really are. We're intelligent people, we're attractive people, we're caring people, we're *healthy* people, and we're proud of who we are.

Our enemies are always pounding away at negative stereotypes, so I'd like to answer a few of them right here, before god and everyone. They say that gay people are sex maniacs. Unfortunately this is not true. I speak from deep, personal experience.

Our enemies say that all lesbians are man-haters. Wrong. The only women who hate men are battered wives. Our enemies say that we're gay because we're incapable of loving the opposite sex. Wrong again. I think we're capable of love in all of its manifestations, and the only people who are queer are the people who can't love anybody.

These stereotypes are ludicrous, but that they are powerful. I think in some ways they helped to influence the recent loathsome Supreme Court decision [Hardwick v. Bowers]. If things were different, if some of those justices knew who we really were, they wouldn't be so quick to condemn us.

And by the way, can you bear that basic black drag? I mean it's not even worn with good pearls!

Justice White, in his majority opinion kept referring to Christian traditions, saying that these traditions made homosexuality unacceptable to most Americans, as well as most people everywhere. I think perhaps he is mistaken, because those same Christian traditions allow wife beating, infanticide and slavery. Suffering is such an important part of Christianity, they seem to feel it's their duty to spread it around. Is this what we have to look forward to with this Supreme Court?

I say we take the Supreme Court and throw them in the Pacific, and if they can walk on water, we believe 'em.

I take great offense at Christianity being bantered about that way. I became a lesbian out of devout Christian charity. All those women out there are praying for a man and I've given them my share! I'm also furious at being accused of single-handedly converting woman to lesbianism. How *wrong* they are. It takes *both* hands.

But you know, you can measure your success by the reactions against you. Obviously we *have* been successful. Pushing and pulling, fighting and screaming, and socks in the jaw are all just part of politics.

This is not a time to run away, this is not a time to pop your integrity in reverse and go back into the closet. This is the time to come forward, to show who you are, and to fight—fight the good fight. It's the only way changes are ever made. Look around you. This is your community and I think you're keeping good company.

So these Gay Games are not just a celebration of skill, they're a celebration of who we are and what we can become. It's a celebration of the best in us. It's a celebration of courage because all the athletes, whether straight or gay, had to overcome a certain amount of prejudice. They had to brave public opinion to come here. If *they* can do it, *we* can do it.

I applaud each of you for being here. I know you have had an individual journey that's all your own, and it was often painful. But you're here, we're all together, we're one family and we're all we've got. So I say, 'Come on, we're all in the same boat, let's pick up an oar and row.'

PHOTO GRAPHICS/DARLENE

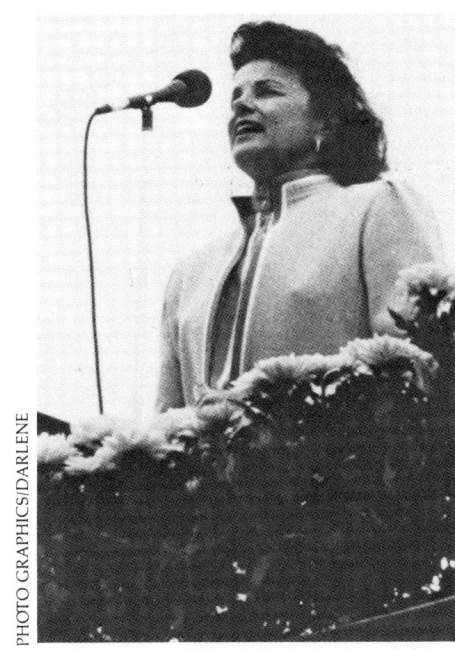

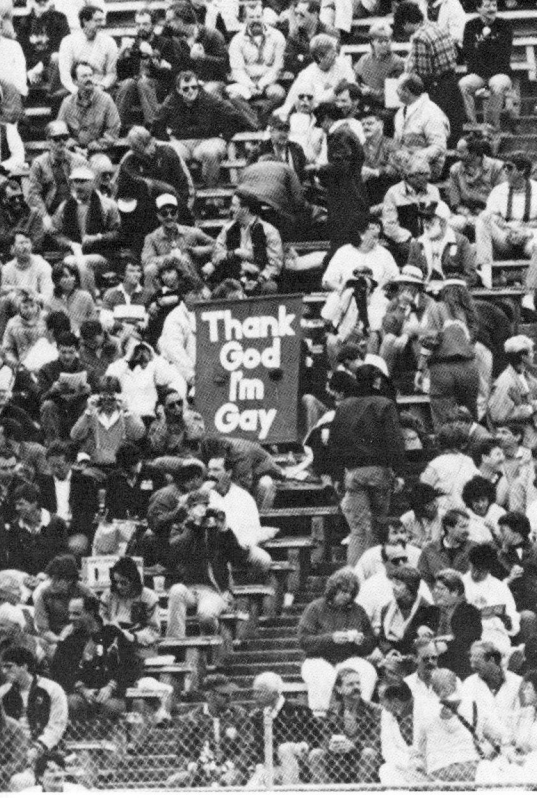

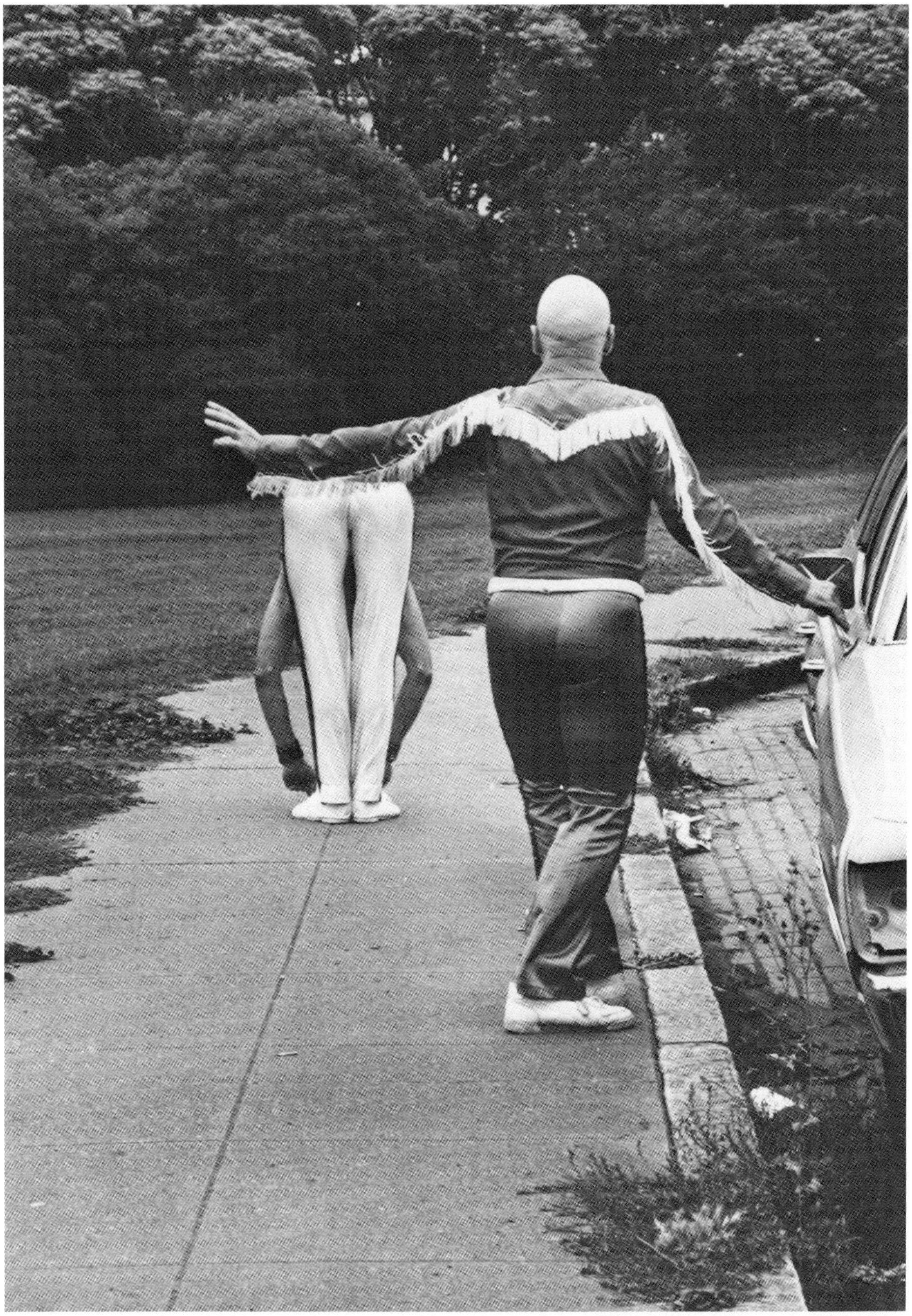

*(Top) San Francisco Mayor Diane Feinstein. (Above, right) Baton twirlers limber up. (Right) The Golden Gate Precision Dancers.*

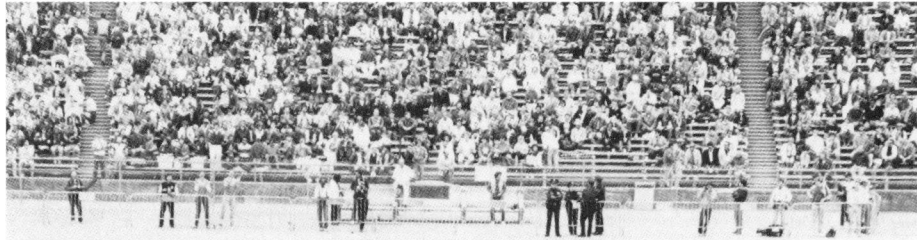

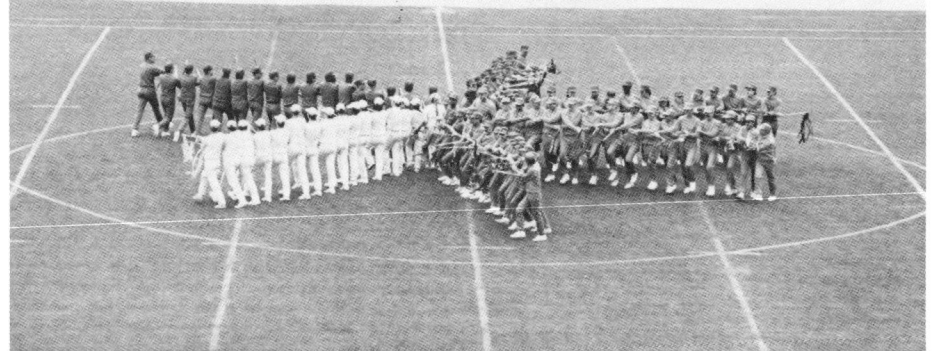

"One of the things that has been a privilege for me to see in San Francisco is the spirit and the talent that rests within the gay community, both men and women. Special spirit, special talent, a coming together in times of trial. And that spirit must continue.

Please feel so welcome to our city and I hope that the Games are the best ever!"
—Diane Feinstein
Mayor, City and County of San Francisco

Today, and for this week, we see ourselves as we really are: active, productive, creative and healthy. And I hope that for this week, and for evermore, we experience the dignity that is the natural consequence of all the activities we're involved in.

### Let the Games begin!

Dr. Tom Waddell
August 9, 1986

The Story of Gay Games II

## PROFILES

*"Sports is one area in the gay community where people can come and know they're being judged for who they are as people, and not for their sexuality. It's very important to see that work, and to know that I had a part in bringing all these men and women together."*

# Sara Lewinstein

### CO-DIRECTOR OF SPORTS □
### SAN FRANCISCO, CALIFORNIA □

"Artemis comes from Greek mythology, and relates to the Roman goddess Diana, one of the four daughters of Zeus. Because she's the only one who did not marry, she was known as the Lesbian Goddess. She was a very strong woman who taught archery, and was also known as the Mother, for being very motherly, yet not married. Many followed her in the tradition of learning different sports."

Meet Sara Lewinstein, owner of the Artemis Cafe. Sara's association with the gay games goes back many years. When approached to help organize bowling for Gay Games I, she assumed that it was "just another men's group" and "refused to be anyone's token." But her curiosity prevailed and she met Tom Waddell and Mark Brown, the primary movers behind the gay games concept. Soon she was a liaison into the women's community for the Games, then co-chair of bowling, and finally a Board member.

She recalls the wild days in the summer of 1982. "There were things that got done, but *how* they got done! It was crazy, but I wouldn't give it up for the world. It was exciting, a very jazzed craziness, seeing that it was all going to work."

Sara's participation in the Games is the culmination of a long commitment to sports. Athletics came naturally while growing up, first in Montreal and then in Los Angeles.

"As a woman it was very hard at the time, breaking into sports. From being a little girl to being a teenager, it started becoming more difficult. The tomboy image, being harassed for that, and now you're a young woman, you should be dating and give up sports. It was very hard for me to consider that."

Later she moved to San Francisco, worked at the Park Bowl and soon became its General Manager. (Park Bowl hosted the bowling and pool events in Gay Games I and II.) She once bowled professionally but it didn't suit her style: "It was very stressful and very conservative. You had to be in a nice skirt, you know, a blouse with your name and city on it, clean white shoes and nylons, no pants were allowed. A lot of the gay women involved were very closeted."

Sara's extensive work in sports extends to softball. She sponsors a women's team through the Artemis Cafe and serves as president of the Park and Recreation Softball Advisory Board. Her association with the first Games led to her position as Co-Director of Sports for Gay Games II.

Hal Herkenhoff, her male counterpart, offers a striking contrast. As Hal stressed the logistical details, Sara added the emotion and the spirit. Together, they shared the enormous responsibility for seventeen sports in all. The chemistry worked: "We've grown to love each other," Sara says without hesitation. "We trust each other enormously and we do complement each other."

She enjoys another special relationship with a man, none other than Tom Waddell. While the two worked side by side in 1982, Sara approached Tom about co-parenting a child. "I was very nervous because I didn't know what his response might be, about taking that risk. I told him I'd been watching him for the last year and I asked him to think it over.

"The response he gave me about how he felt towards children put tears in my eyes. It was exactly how I felt. He was just like me, except a guy. He felt the same way about sports, about bringing people together."

Soon after the Games, Tom and Sara conceived Jessica, who turned three years old just before Gay Games II. "I call her my little miracle that happened from a miracle, because I think pulling off Gay Games I was a true miracle and deserves being recognized as such. Then having Jessica was something I always wanted."

In the gay and lesbian community, her commitment to sports is exemplary. "To me, the Gay Games is a school for teaching. We're all students at times and I still consider myself a student. But with the Games I also feel very much the teacher. Teaching love and prosperity through that, and sharing.

"Sports is one area in the gay community where people can come and know they're being judged for who they are as people, and not for their sexuality. It's very important to see that work, and to know that I had a part in bringing all these men and women together." □

A Sense of Pride:

# PROFILES

*"I look at my job as providing people with a real opportunity to create a larger community."*

# Hal Herkenhoff

☐ CO-DIRECTOR OF SPORTS

☐ SAN FRANCISCO, CALIFORNIA

From 6:00 to 8:00 AM each morning during Games week, Hal Herkenhoff stayed at home to field telephone calls and plan his schedule. Then he was on the move all day, racing between sport venues to deliver supplies and resolve problems. His other duty, which brought considerably more pleasure, was to help award medals to inspired gay men and women.

"We knew that the first days of competition would be the hardest," Hal relates. "But once the first day of bowling, for example, was over you could be sure that the rest would go smoothly."

Along with Derek Liecty, Director of Facilities, Hal was the keeper of schedules, tending to the infinite number of details involved in staging the sporting events of Gay Games II.

Hal is businesslike and straightforward, the perfect complement to his ebullient co-chair, Sara Lewinstein. "We're quite a contrast," Hal admits. "But I think the way our talents have balanced each other has been a major plus in putting the sports program together. "I don't really have any emotional attachment to the Games," Hal goes on. "I look at my job as providing people with a real opportunity to create a larger community."

No emotional attachment? It seems hard to believe.

"I've managed huge catering jobs, a thousand people and the like," Hal explains. "The Games fits right into the progression of what I've been doing: catering, logistics, personnel management. The Gay Games are just a multiple-day, multiple-event festival. I've never handled this many sites, but here there are just people and equipment. No perishables, no service design."

Hal has been involved in competitive swimming for twenty-five years. It began in San Jose, California after moving north from Trona, a tiny town near Death Valley. Hal competed through junior high and high school. When he showed interest in joining the Santa Clara Swim Club (SCSC), his parents balked.

SCSC was well known as the premier training club on the west coast, where swimmers like Mark Spitz (gold medalist in the 1968 and 1972 Olympics) had been groomed. To Hal, his parents' decision meant that he would remain at a "middle level forever."

A flicker of resentment can be heard in his voice. "I didn't burn out because I was never pushed, and my parents didn't allow me to push myself that much. It was always kept recreational."

Hal went to Berkeley during the Vietnam protest years. Ronald Reagan was governor and ordered troops and tear gas onto the campus. Hal recalls this as "a weird time," yet found the opportunity to organize the fraternity league in swimming. Along the way he met a man from Hawaii at the pool who seduced him. "One, two, three," Hal says with a smile. "It was so easy."

Gay Games I was the first chance for Hal to get back into competitive swimming. Like so many athletes who excel in college, his years after Berkeley involved little exercise. "There is a chain, as one affects the other, between competition and workouts. You go back and forth. You find that one helps the other. You need real goals to keep moving on."

After winning medals in 1982, Hal was inspired to stay on as a volunteer with SFAA. He and Sara were named Co-directors of Sports in January 1984. The months before Gay Games II went by fast. For a long time the sports committees were the only sign of life outside of board meetings.

The biggest challenge throughout was to motivate people "to deal with the reality of our situation, the shortages of money and lack of support in other areas. You needed to keep them from getting discouraged, and focused on handling tasks and deadlines."

Hal credits the chemistry with Sara for much of their success. "We needed to have such thorough communication, and such a similar line of sight towards this goal. The two of us had to provide mutual patience, understanding and intensity."

With their own unique skills and styles, Hal and Sara pulled together a strong committee structure. All told, they helped stage seventy event-days of competition in seventeen sports, the core activity of Gay Games II.  ☐

The Story of Gay Games II

A Sense of Pride:

# Basketball

The Story of Gay Games II

## Profiles

*"I am flattered to be at the Gay Games, and it is an honor for me to run against other gay people. This event shows the world that we're just like everybody else. We are not alone."*

# Jeff Ryan

BASKETBALL, TRACK & FIELD □

SYDNEY, AUSTRALIA □

A full court basketball game was underway in the Sydney city league. The match was physical and intense. There was obvious enmity, and elbows flew, filling the lane in front of the net. Verbal challenges could be heard above the din. The gay men's team trailed at half time, but pulled out the game with a scoring burst at the close.

I was constantly reminded: this team plays in a straight men's league. The previous year they had won the championship. "We had about sixty spectators cheering us on," remembers Jeff Ryan. "The competition had only about ten. All the screaming and going on at the court when we won—it was a lovely feeling. "No doubt the losers were a bit angry over their defeat to a team of "poofs" (an Australian slang term for gays).

Jeff is team captain for basketball and was responsible for bringing them to the Gay Games. It was hard to convince many of the players that the expense would be worth it (it runs about $1200 for round trip airfare). "I kept pounding into everybody's head that this would be the experience of a lifetime. 'You'll enjoy it, you'll have fun and you'll meet a lot of people. If you win, fine. But just being there to compete will be good for your own self-esteem.'"

The hub of gay activity in Sydney, as in most other cities, is the thriving bar scene. Slowly, leaders like Jeff Ryan are helping to expose people to healthier alternatives. As a lifetime Sydney resident, he "had never seen much activity in sport until the last two years. It's been quite dormant. I know people have been playing sport, but not openly, as I wanted to play."

Jeff and I met in the small apartment he shares with his lover of two years, Richard. It was hard to believe that this space could contain his restless energy, not to mention his long legs. Yet everything was compact and in its place. The building was one of several brick structures that hugged a hill overlooking downtown Sydney. A few blocks away was the gym where Jeff works out.

He has always been athletic, "sporty" in Australian lingo. His high point during school came when he was chosen for the Australian level rubgy union team—similar to our "all-American" status.

For Gay Games II Jeff began an intense six-day workout schedule, which included coaching the men's league, weight training and running. He competed in basketball as well as track and field.

He enjoyed success in his track events and won a gold medal in the high jump, along with a silver in the 400 meters. He anchored the Sydney relay team which won medals (with no prior practice) in both the 4 x 100 (four men, each running 100 meters) and 4 x 200 events.

"I am flattered to be at the Gay Games," Jeff told me, "and it is an honor for me to run against other gay people. This event shows the world that we're just like everybody else. We are not alone." □

# Billiards

38                                                                                          A Sense of Pride:

# Soccer

JEANNETTE EGGER

A Sense of Pride:

# Bowling

CATHY CADE

# Cycling

A Sense of Pride:

# PROFILES

*"While cycling, I am aware of the outside, but I am completely within myself and it's nice. It taps inner strengths and inner energies that I didn't know were there before."*

# Patsy Lynch

☐ CYCLING

☐ WASHINGTON, D.C.

Pert, aggressive, independent, Patsy Lynch has set certain personal and professional goals. At age thirty-two, she is bound and determined to meet them. And can she talk a blue streak!

"I was a tomboy at the age of two. I laugh because I've read studies that say there's a correlation between women who are involved in sports and homosexuality. If that's the case, I'm a prime example. I've been competing in sports since I was about six or seven... I was a jock before it was fashionable for a woman to be a jock."

She once played tackle football. In grade school and high school she ran the 880 in track and cross-country, then played varsity field hockey and volleyball. As a kid she also rode dressage for ten years in competition. Patsy kept her parents busy nearly every weekend as they drove their eldest daughter around the Washington, DC area competing in various events.

After college she began graduate school, and dove into a totally different sport. "I rediscovered rugby—I say rediscovered because early in college I dated this guy for a while who was a rugby player, and went to a lot of games with him. I was told that women couldn't possibly play rugby, and I decided that was bullshit."

She played a total of six years on various teams. A high point came when her team from the Washington area went on tour with a team from Boston to London and Wales.

"The women [in England] were appalled. The men were enthusiastic. One of the arguments was that if women played rugby it would hurt their innards—their reproductive organs [laugh]—and they would be unable to have children, which in my case is perfectly fine. We found out later that one of the women on my team was pregnant and later had a healthy baby boy."

If one were to attempt to classify Patsy as feminist, or lesbian, or butch (she wears her hair cropped short), it would not do justice to her thoughtful reflections on women's roles. Commenting on her rugby days, she recalls:

"Most of the women I played against were gay, but not all of them. There was more tolerance, I think, among athletes. It was not an issue of gay vs. straight. It was simply women athletes playing together. Our sexual orientation was not important."

In fact, the subject of roles recurred several times over the course of our interview. It is striking that Patsy herself has chosen to be out front on women's issues, in her own non-conformist way. She cares little for what other lesbians think about her activities, and freely admits that her activities ignore the traditional separation of gay men and lesbians.

"I find that the 'separatist' ideas exclude a part of myself, since I consider myself androgynous. I have equal aspects of male and female in my personality.

"If I decide I want something, I'm going to get it. After working professionally as a photographer for ten years, I've finally started to get more work. A lot of it's just tenacity and the fact that I'm willing to take chances, risks."

Cycling is now the primary sport which gives an outlet for this fierce determination. Like running or swimming, it requires long hours of training—most of them alone. In training for the Games, Patsy began a regimen that peaked at 400-500 miles of road work *per week*. She also works on weight and circuit training.

Patsy avoids the term "loner," preferring instead to speak of her personal motivation. You have to wonder, though, if athletics and her professional career alone can satisfy in the long run.

"While cycling, I am aware of the outside, but I am completely within myself and it's nice. It taps inner strengths and inner energies that I didn't know were there before. It is refreshing.

"If some woman that I love has rejected me, I can remove myself from that and take myself to a place where I have a chance to just assess what's going on, come to terms with it, and realize that it is just one more step in my development. It keeps me going." ☐

The Story of Gay Games II

# Diving

The Story of Gay Games II

## PROFILES

*"I think gay people need to identify ourselves to one another, to show that we are supportive of each other, and to create a dialogue with other people out there."*

# Dana Cox

□ SWIMMING

□ SEATTLE, WASHINGTON

**The setting:** Tacoma, Washington, fall of 1982. You are tuned to KTNT radio, with talk show host Dr. Wayne Johnson. His guest: Dana Cox, gold medal winner at Gay Games I. Dr. Johnson begins the show by asking listeners whether they would object to having the second Gay Games held at the recently completed Tacoma Dome, a local sports arena.

**Caller #1:** I am opposed to anything which is destructive to the foundation of this nation, which is the American family.

**Dr. Johnson:** Are you opposed to the gay community having an athletic event?

**Caller #1:** Make any assumptions you want. If gay promotes family life, I'm for it. If it's destructive to the foundation of this civilization, which is the family, which consists of mother, father and children, the strength of the nation, then I'm opposed to that.

**Dr. Johnson:** Which do you think it is? Is it destructive to the family or does it promote the family?

**Caller #1:** Do you think being gay promotes family life?

**Dana:** I feel very supportive of families. It's a very necessary part of the perpetuation of the race.

**Caller #1:** Then whatre you doing to perpetuate the race?

**Dana:** Ma'am, I don't need to do anything. I think there is plenty of room for all of us. In fact, I think we offer a real good birth control alternative.

**Caller #2:** If this world continues as it is today and escalates, you see more gays and more crime and everything. The subject was discussed this morning about the atomic bomb—I say, come on and bring the bombs in.

**Dr. Johnson:** Mr. Cox, he's saying that you're symptomatic of an erosion of morals that will lead to the decline of western civilization.

**Dana:** There have always been homosexuals; there has always been homosexuality. I think the reason we are seeing more of it now is because of an increase in the tolerance of society which is allowing people to come out and be open about their choice, as I am.

**Dr. Johnson:** So you see tolerance as a sign that society is maturing?

**Dana:** Yes.

**Caller #3:** I just called to apologize for those people in my age bracket who are so narrow-minded that they can't see that people who are classified as gay are indeed human beings, and I have known many who are very, very fine people. It turns my stomach when people are intolerant.

**Caller #4:** If you had studied the Bible you'd know how much that type of living is condemned . . . .

**Caller #5:** I'm so tired of all these would-be Christians. It is said, "Judge not, lest you be judged." I am not of the gay persuasion myself, but they have a right to do what they want to, and they will answer to their own conscience and their own God for it.

**Caller #6:** This is a very controversial subject. I am against the practice of homosexuality, but gays have their rights . . . . Nobody has to know that they're gay. As long as they're not hurting anybody and nobody knows what they're doing behind their own closed doors, they can do what they want. I do not think they should be out practicing openly or holding special olympics.

**Dana:** I don't want to go into the closet, those closed doors that he is talking about. I think it is important for people to understand, and I want the freedom to express myself. He certainly has the right to turn me off, but I think gay people need to identify ourselves to one another, to show that we are supportive of each other, and to create a dialogue with other people out there.

\* \* \*

Dana Cox deserves a lot of credit for his efforts to bring gay issues into the open. He survived this radio show in 1982 and went on to swim with Team Seattle in Gay Games II. He earned a bronze in the 200 yard breast stroke, and achieved three personal best times overall. Dana lives with his lover David in Seattle.

A Sense of Pride:

"In the triathlon, you are often just dead-tired. But I'm not a quitter. If I set a goal, if I see it as a challenge, I'll carry through with it."
—Jeff Keeny
San Diego, California

# Triathlon

The Story of Gay Games II

A Sense of Pride:

The Story of Gay Games II 53

PROFILES

*"I spend many hours running. Sometimes it's been running away from, but now it's running towards something. It's running towards love, compassion, caring and spirituality, towards my health and well-being. There's been a nice turn, a nice change."*

# Bart Hopple

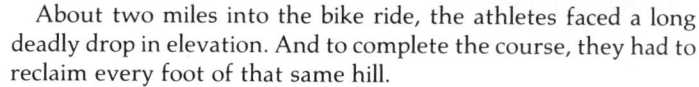

TRIATHLON, SWIMMING □

SAN DIEGO, CALIFORNIA □

In the first leg of the triathlon, a half-mile swim, Joe Weaver was first to dash from the cold water of Lake Anza, followed closely by Bart Hopple, both from San Diego. Ian Nash, an Australian, trailed in third.

The transition area was roped off from spectators. Bicycles, shoes and clothing had been carefully laid out by each participant. The triathletes raced to their gear, changed clothes, and were off on a twenty mile cycling course through the sweeping hills east of Berkeley.

Cycling is Bart Hopple's strongest sport. Off he went, pedaling fast with a grim look of determination. The cycling course was grueling, which appealed to Bart's sense of aesthetics.

"Hills are my favorite part," he states, contrary to the sentiments of most athletes. "They're a challenge that makes me feel alive. People who ride with me know that I'll lose them as soon as the climb begins. It is my personal goal to just sit there and push it. Before it was driven by fear. Now it's driven by training."

About two miles into the bike ride, the athletes faced a long deadly drop in elevation. And to complete the course, they had to reclaim every foot of that same hill.

It was no surprise when Bart Hopple passed his teammate from San Diego and finished the bike segment in the lead. With a quick change of shoes, he was off on the final leg, a six mile run.

Bart dedicated this race to his mother, who was dying. He told me beforehand that he would win. Not that he *thought* he would win, but that he *would* win.

Cocky? To be sure. Bart wanted this victory more than anything else in the world. The bravado was the mask of someone who is always pushing himself to the limit. The triathlon attracts a certain breed of athlete. You can't help but wonder what motivates someone like Bart Hopple to train so hard for so long.

"Staying alive," he says simply. "Being healthy, being thin. I am one of ten children, and I have sisters and brothers who top 300-400 pounds. A person who does the triathlon tends to be on the obsessive side." Perhaps the relentless force that keeps Bart driving forward will be tempered some day as a result of his accomplishments ... if he could only relax long enough to enjoy them.

True to his word, Bart finished the triathlon with a gold medal in his age group, 30-34. He placed second overall, with the Australian Ian Nash passing him in the final running leg.

Two weeks later Bart flew to Ohio to visit his dying mother and say goodbye. Soon thereafter, she passed away.

"I spend many hours running. Sometimes it's been running away from, but now it's running towards something. It's running towards love, compassion, caring and spirituality, towards my health and well-being. There's been a nice turn, a nice change." □

ROY COE

# Softball

# PROFILES

*"I don't like lying and I don't like hiding."*

# Sue Williams

☐ SOFTBALL

☐ HONOLULU, HAWAII

Sue Williams remembers the day she donned a player's uniform for the first time for the softball team she coached. After hard work with brand new players in the Honolulu area, the team had gelled into a cohesive unit. But that day they were one player shy and nearly had to forfeit the game. "You guys want me to be a player/coach? Can you handle that? Do you want me to put myself in the batting order wherever I want?"

As shortstop in that game, Sue went four for four, turned a couple of double plays, and played errorless ball. Her team was thrilled—they nearly won their first game.

For Sue, the intensity of athletics has cooled off. She used to put in hours of hard practice and long playing hours at school back in Oregon. In Hawaii, the pace is slower, the mood more sociable. She appreciates the change.

"Since I've been over here, I just got back on my feet. It's so comfortable. There is so much 'Aloha,' so much family love. You can accomplish a lot as a loving individual. I have a short temper but now I can control it. It has been so nice here for the past three years."

For Gay Games II, Sue eased away from coaching and played outfield for the Honolulu team. While they did not place in the top three for the softball tournament, the women enjoyed themselves tremendously.

Sue freely acknowleges the rebel side of her personality. From childhood she's played the role of tomboy, even to the point of backing up her brother in school fights. Sue was always the first to organize a game of baseball or football in the neighborhood.

Her physical prowess served her well on the playing field and she secured an athletic scholorship at the University of Nevada in two sports: volleyball and softball. Later she attended the University of Oregon in Eugene. This was more rewarding to Sue as an athlete, since Oregon was a stronger team. As shortstop Sue played with the team during the Collegiate World Series in Oklahoma where they finished seventh overall.

Significant changes came about during her time in Eugene. For one thing, she realized her need for female intimacy. A close friend, Jackie, came out and became attached to another woman. Watching her friend develop a lesbian relationship prompted Sue to seek her own companion.

To her first lover, she said, "Teach me. I want to know everything. Tell me now!" Sue recalls vividly, "I didn't go home for five days...."

Leaving college, Sue pursued a longtime ambition: to coach softball. Her team, from North Eugene High School, played "flawlessly, all year round." She took this group of women to the Oregon state championships.

Still restless, Sue moved to Honolulu where she has been for the past three years. She is now more at ease with the world and has finally come out to her family. This was a long process which began with her brother George with whom she has always felt a special bond.

Since living on the islands, she has come out to her parents as well. "I got tired of my father saying, 'When are you going to get married? You should go down to the university, hang around the engineering department and get a guy.'

"Now my family knows, and I realize that this was the element that was missing in our relationship—because I don't like lying and I don't like hiding." ☐

CATHY CADE

The Story of Gay Games II

"We were playing in a gay softball tournament and I was surprised to see that my father had come to watch. He tapped me on the shoulder and said, 'Are all these people gay?' I told him, 'Yes, they are.' It opened his eyes to the fact that being gay doesn't change your physical appearance. You can just be yourself and people don't ever know what your sexual preference is."
—Troy Bronstein
San Diego, California

A Sense of Pride:

# Physique

The Story of Gay Games II

The Story of Gay Games II

MICK HICKS

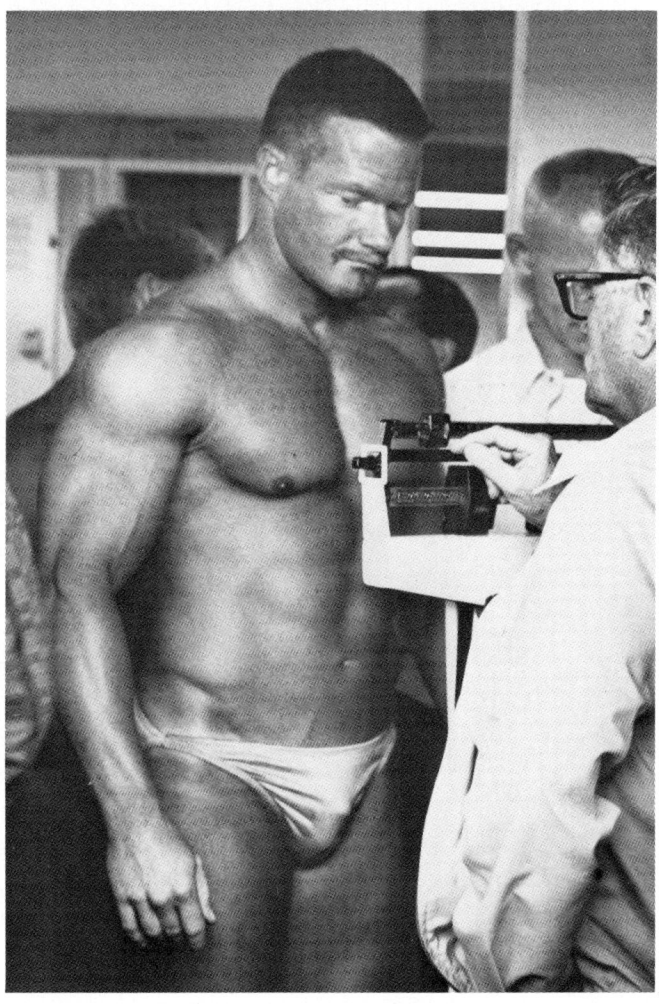

# PROFILES

*"I know this is the year. Let's do it. Let's go! I can't wait!"*

# Nitra Allen

☐ PHYSIQUE

☐ SACRAMENTO, CALIFORNIA

At her first body building event, the California state championship, Nitra was overwhelmed by the thrill of performance: "Until you actually experience it, you can't put it into words. I think of all the time I've put in, the eight months at the gym six or seven days a week. The results were worth it, but it couldn't have prepared me for going out on that stage with three or four thousand howling, screaming drooling people. Pitch black, and you can't see a thing!"

Nitra works with other body builders in a small gym. She began her athletic career in track and field, and once competed as an all-American javelin thrower. Once she began training in Olympic style weightlifting, however, she considered her physique and the die was cast.

As a professional tradesman, where intolerance for women runs high, Nitra is careful to keep her work life and private life separate. At home, her time is hectic since she works daytime hours and lifts weights at other times. She gives a lot of credit to her lover Maria "for being there every step of the way, consoling me and getting my diet right, fixing me meals and keeping me in there."

The two are also are also raising Nitra's young son, Nehemiah. They affectionately call him "our son" and share in the parental responsibilities. Maria brought Nehemiah to Opening Ceremonies to watch Nitra march in with her Sacramento teammates.

Body building involves a lot more than pushing weights around at the gym. It necessitates a strict regimen regarding diet, exercise and rest. It takes almost fanatical devotion to peak at just the right moment before competition. Months before the Games, Nitra was already psyching herself up for the event.

"You know you're hot when you come into a show. You just know it. You did your diet just right, you trained, your body's symmetrical, nothing is out of proportion.

"This has to be one of the truest forms of athletic expression, because if you're in good condition and everything looks just right, there's nothing more beautiful than a body. It's yours. It's your own expression of how you feel about yourself. I know this is the year. Let's do it. Let's go! I can't wait!"

Most winners in body building at Gay Games II were determined Friday morning by judges, a fact unknown to most of the crowd at Civic Auditorium who came to savor muscles for the evening show of finalists. Nitra won a silver medal in the Light Heavyweight class. Her energetic dance routine, bright smile and marvelous physique were well-appreciated by the crowd.

But the real show-stopper came in the team competition, an event judged solely on the evening performance. Teammates Juan Ramos and Mike Ward joined Nitra in a jazzy routine that brought the house to its feet. The judges agreed: Sacramento took home the gold medal for best team physique.

"It was a great piece of choreography," Nitra told me after the event, "and the three of us had trained together for a long time. You know, we talk to each other now more than ever before. Mike and Juan are both real gentlemen.

"And it was a great feeling to be out there by myself in front of the crowd, out in front of the gay community. I knew the men would get applause, but it was nice to see the crowd also respond so well to the women." ☐

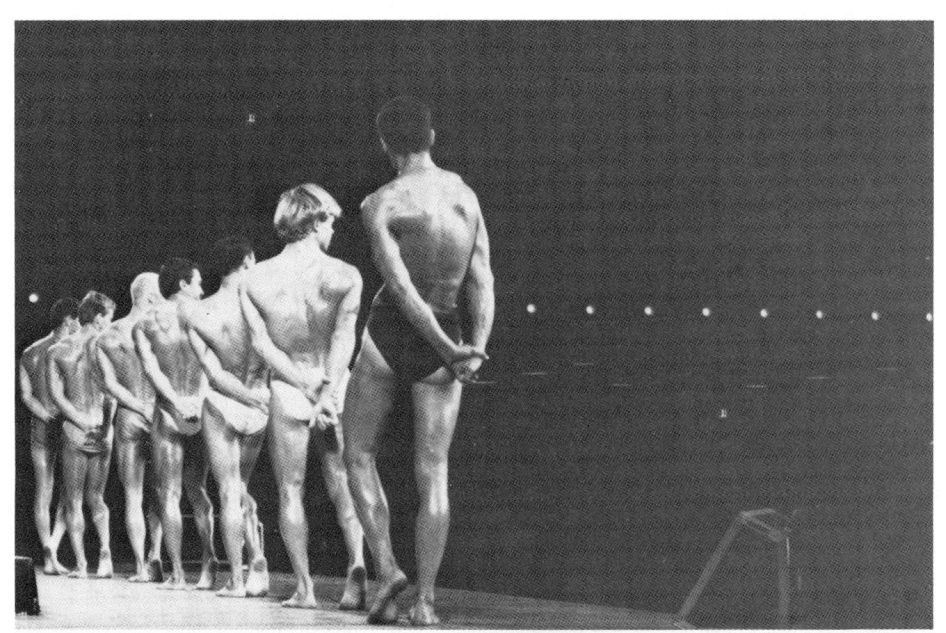

A Sense of Pride:

The Story of Gay Games II

70  A Sense of Pride:

"I attended Gay Games I, but watched as a spectator from the stands. I was furious with myself for not competing. I made up my mind right then and there that I was going to enter the next Games. It made me feel much more a part of the whole experience."
—Owen Shanks
Wellington, New Zealand

# Track & Field

MICK HICKS

The Story of Gay Games II

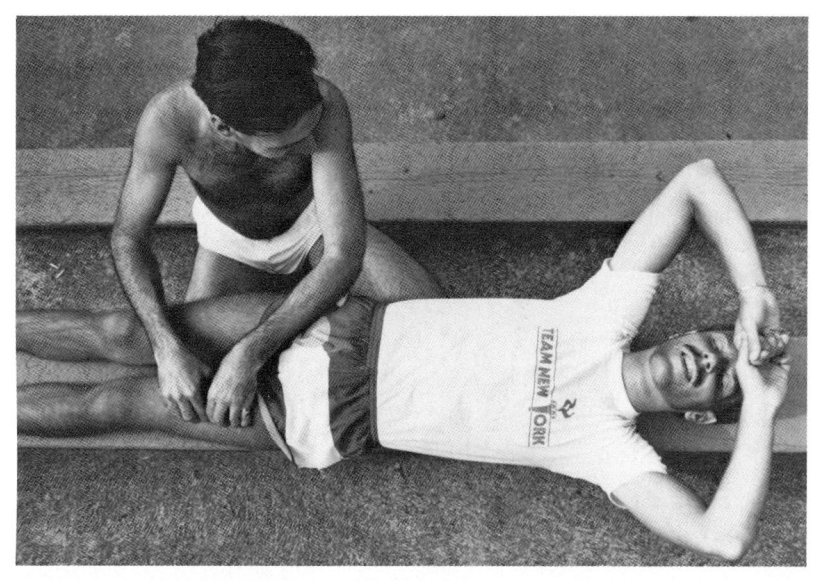

PHOTO GRAPHICS/DARLENE

## PROFILES

*"Running makes me feel like I am still young. It is a challenge, and I don't really challenge myself in a lot of other areas in life."*

# Fern Antipol

☐ TRACK & FIELD

☐ WASHINGTON, D.C.

In Gay Games I, Fern Antipol was the only woman from Washington, DC to participate. In 1986 she joined twenty-four other atheletes from the capital for the trip to San Francisco for Gay Games II.

She corresponded regularly with the Games office in that four year interim. Her entry in track, along with her lover Carol's in racquetball, was among the very first to be received for Gay Games II. On top of that, she was eager to be interviewed.

When you meet Fern, you know right off that she is the genuine article: friendly, earnest and straightforward. She began running to keep fit nine years ago. Her workout is recreational. She doesn't push herself, but runs to keep in shape.

In the first Games she ran the 5 and 10K races. In 1986 she ran just the 5K. Her perseverance in the face of much faster competition is an example of the Gay Games philosophy that participation in sports is the true reward.

"Running makes me feel like I am still young. It is a challenge, and I don't really challenge myself in a lot of other areas in life. At first, I would say, 'Look, I can run five miles,' and then I'd take an hour to do it.

"In the first Games, I ran 3.1 miles in about twenty-five minutes. For me that was fabulous, because my fastest time before was a nine minute mile." In her indefatigable style, she notes that she loses "about a minute a year."

At Gay Games II, Fern admits that she was disappointed with her performance. "Yet I learned a lot about running a race. Next time, I'll know how to be better prepared."

Fern moved to Washington from the Bronx, New York where she was raised and went to high school. She now works as a legal secretary in the capital. She has developed a sense of security in this environment, and holds her own against the men who work as partners in the firm.

She originally moved south to have her first relationsip with another woman. After breaking up, she went through a period of "just finding out that I could take care of myself. I may prefer to be with someone else, but I can survive by myself quite nicely. That was real important."

Fern and Carol have been together for two years, and were inseparable during Gay Games II. One can tell that things are going strong. I saw them several times—at the Opening, at the track stadium, at the swimming competition. They were quite a pair, and always dressed in the blue uniforms emblazened with *WASHINGTON, DC*.

"I don't see where people get the idea that gay people won't stay together," she says from the heart. "I don't see why it should be different—except there are no papers, no real legal commitment. I go by my feelings." ☐

The Story of Gay Games II

## PROFILES

*"Everyone started looking at us as if we were the Soviet team or something. They must have been amazed. We were asked the most ridiculous questions, like 'are there gay people in Ireland?'"*

# Oliver Murphy

☐ DECATHLON

☐ DUBLIN, IRELAND

"We used to get magazines from a German weekly (my mother is German), and one of them did a series on West German hopefuls for the Mexico City Olympics in 1968. They did a full series on the decathlon team. There were five or six guys in this training camp and they were all photographed.

"This was high altitude training in Switzerland. It was beside a lake, and the lake was blue, and the sky was blue, and the mountains were white, and the grass was green, and all these guys were bronzed and gorgeous. I thought, 'My God, this is what I want to be. And *this* is decathlon!'"

Oliver Murphy, then 17 years old, measured off 100 meters on the road with the help of his father, then 400 meters, and 1500 meters, and he began to run. He felled trees to fashion a javelin to throw and a pole to vault with. He collected stones from the seashore for the shot-put and the discus. "Every spare minute I had," he recalls, "I trained and trained and trained."

Once at the University in Cork, Oliver was in heaven. They had a track and field club along with all-weather facilities. He continued to train and compete at the county and provincial level, ultimately reaching the national championships. His performance steadily improved and he regularly placed in the top ten.

A small item in the London Gay News heralded the first "Gay Olympic Games." Oliver wrote and received his call to action. "Did you ever dream you could be marching into a stadium as a member of your team?" the literature read. Like a fairy tale come true, Oliver and two friends were on their way to San Francisco in August of 1982.

Their arrival at the Registration Center caused a stir. The Irish men had arrived! "Everyone started looking at us as if we were the Soviet team or something. They must have been amazed. We were asked the most ridiculous questions, like 'are there gay people in Ireland?'"

After nine grueling events in the decathlon at Gay Games I, competitors faced the final 1500 meter race. Oliver led by several hundred points over his nearest rival. After one lap he took the lead and began to move out further and further.

"I always dreamed about what it must be like at the big games, to come into the final straight in the 1500 and know you have won. That was without a doubt, emotionally, the high point of my life. There is nothing that has ever happened to me as fantastic as those 15 to 20 seconds going down the home stretch."

In the four years since Gay Games I, Oliver has settled down in San Francisco. He lives with his lover David, a "track and field widow." Oliver's fiber glass pole leans along one wall (they have to navigate it down the fire escape). The shot-put and discus are stashed in the bedroom, the starting blocks in Oliver's huge duffel bag. David has nicknamed his lover "Imelda" (after Imelda Marcos of the Philippines) since he has a different pair of training shoes for nearly all ten events.

The Gay Games office received a letter in July 1986 which read, "Today my package of registration papers arrived. For the first time since the closing ceremonies of the first games, I cried and cried and cried. To all of you who work behind the scenes to make this wonderful dream a reality, my heartfelt thanks — O. G. Murphy."

For Gay Games II, Oliver once again marched into the stadium with an Irish flag. Both his mother and his lover David watched proudly as Oliver won the gold medal for the decathlon in his age group and finished second overall. He scored a personal best in the pole vault, clearing nine feet.

Modestly, Oliver explains that his love for decathlon stems from a sense of aesthetics. "I go to the gym and see these guys with huge triceps and huge pecs, and it offends me in a way. My idea of a muscle is something that's working. You *do* something with it. It's really a Greek idea, the notion of using your body to do beautiful things. A really good athlete with a really good technique is beautiful to look at.

"For me, throwing a javelin is a beautiful thing." ☐

## Profiles

*"I decided I wouldn't have a midlife crisis, but midlife madness instead—and this is part of it!"*

# Mac McMahon

TRACK, VOLLEYBALL □

SYDNEY, AUSTRALIA □

"My aim is to change the statistics. I don't want people to believe that ten or twenty or fifty percent of the people who have come in contact with AIDS necessarily go on to get a related condition, or AIDS itself. No one is giving people that message. That's what I am fighting to get across."

Mac McMahon, volleyball player, community volunteer and holistic practitioner, has dedicated a great deal of his life and energy towards helping others in the gay community. As an acupuncturist and counselor, he faces the uphill battle of overcoming traditional attitudes in Sydney, Australia.

Introducing naturalistic concepts into people's lifestyles is not easy. He has trained with "Ankali," an AIDS support group in Sydney similar to the Shanti Project in San Francisco. Ankali is an aboriginal word meaning "friend."

Most of his clients have reached out to him as a last resort, when traditional medicine failed to offer answers ... or hope. "I tell them to think about what their doctors have told them. I try to say, 'You have an alternative. You may not have to take the chemotherapies and the experimental drugs and things that further impair your immune system. You can do it on your own, with help, with support, and using natural methods.'

"They always come to me feeling that they're going to die. After an hour and a half of talking to me, they walk out knowing that they have a chance to live—which is where I get my kicks out of it, I suppose. It makes it worthwhile, knowing you've changed something in these people."

Mac was born in England. Later his family emigrated to Adelaide in South Australia. In 1969 he moved to Sydney. "Up until then I was struggling to find my identity. It was very uncomfortable and frightening. Then in Sydney I went to a gay dance and saw 600 other gay men and women having a good time. I said, 'Bingo. It's okay. You're okay.'"

He spent some time in Europe, which he calls his "finishing school," then returned to Sydney and enrolled in a four year course at the New South Wales College of Natural Therapies.

His studies led him to acupuncture. A six month tour of duty in a Chinese hospital rounded out this education. Mac's fascination for holistic routines continues to this day. He calls himself a "lifestyle consultant," using a variety of techniques, including acupuncture, to help his predominantly gay clientele.

Mac realized that he needed to apply this knowledge to his own life. He cut out drugs and moderated his drinking. He began to pay close attention to the foods he ate and the way he cared for his spiritual health. These changes offered immediate payoffs.

"We all have belief systems, but usually they're in our heads and we don't actually follow through on them. At the moment it seems that I am. Although I'm 42, I am healthier than I've ever been ... being healthy, that is my safeguard. It's going to be the thing that saves me."

Athletics complement this interest in health. Mac jogs, attends two aerobics classes a week, works with weights, and practices with the volleyball team three nights a week. He finds time on occasion to work on yoga, stretching and Tai Chi.

In recognition of his boundless energy, the Sydney men voted Mac their team captain for Gay Games II. Spectators will long remember the Aussies marching into Opening and Closing Ceremonies in native garb, including bush hats, moleskins and boots.

Mac competed in volleyball and track. He won four track medals, including a gold in the 1500 meter run. His times were all personal bests.

"This is absolutely fantastic," he exclaimed. "I decided I wouldn't have a midlife crisis, but midlife *madness* instead—and this is part of it!"

After a long vacation in the states, Mac returns to extensive volunteer work back in Sydney. This includes an "antibody support group" at a local clinic, and immune system workshops.

Still, the battle against AIDS is frustrating: "I feel very sad inside myself that, even in the gay community in Sydney, I can help people only when they take the opportunity to listen. I know it can happen. I feel I have the compassion to love these people. But I have the frustration of nothing happening. Very slowly, in my own way, I'm reaching a few people."

When you meet Mac McMahon for the first time, very little of that sadness shows through. The twinkle in his eye and his earnest manner make you a believer right away. "Miracles happen here sometimes," he says with a smile. "The needles work magic on some people. It's amazing the results after one treatment. Some people don't respond though. It's not 100% effective. But the miracles make it all worthwhile." □

**A Sense of Pride:**

# PROFILES

*"My motto is, 'Respect them all, but fear no one.'"*

# Bernard Turner

☐ TRACK & FIELD

☐ SAN FRANCISCO, CALIFORNIA

Bernard Turner looked around in amazement at the spectacle known as the "Corporate Cup." Bank of America had given him extra money, a uniform, and paid his travel expenses in order that he might be there. Dotting the landscape were brightly colored tents and flags, representing such corporate giants as General Electric and IBM.

"After the finals, they had a big outdoor dance with food, a portable sound system and DJ. Then we went back to the hotel and they threw a party with live music and all the food and booze you could want. And let me tell you, these people got down, you know what I mean? They were real corporate, straight-laced types. I was the only gay guy on my whole team."

This scene was a long way from Chicago where Bernard grew up, where "gay wasn't cool" and "you were either a closet case who got married or a drag queen." Along the way he had served in the Navy, spent four years in Amsterdam and sung vocals in a rock band.

The Corporate Cup was also a far cry from Gay Games I, where Bernard served as co-chair of Track & Field. He met Tom Waddell in 1980 and was encouraged to help other runners train for the event.

Following the first Games, Bernard helped to organize the San Francisco Track & Field Club. Every Sunday, Tuesday and Thursday this group of gay runners trains for Masters competition in meets throughout California. Each year they travel to the Nationals competition to test their mettle. Bernard coaches the team, collects entry forms and acts as all around cheerleader for gay track enthusiasts.

He has been training since 1982 with three other runners, Frank Denby, Rick Thoman and Earl Bryant, fine sprinters in their own right. Together they make up the 4x100 relay team that breezed by the competition to take first place at Gay Games II.

As an athlete in the Games, I trained with the San Francisco Track & Field Club, and watched Bernard coach both men and women. The comaraderie and success of our team is a credit to his enthusiasm and love for the sport.

Bernard is modest, given his own talent (he won five medals at the Games, four of them gold). He takes real pleasure in helping others develop their ability. "I could always go out there for my own personal glory, run just for Bernard Turner and do just as well. But I'd rather run with a team. And if it's a gay team, that makes it even better.

"My motto is, 'Respect them all, but fear no one.' That's what I try to tell the team. If you practice hard, you don't have to be afraid. Even if you don't win, at least you have done your personal best.

"We have men and women who have never run, who are probably not competitive, who train with us and then go out and win. That's the best compliment I can get as coach." ☐

SAVAGE PHOTOGRAPHY

The Story of Gay Games II

## PROFILES

*"The Games have made me proud to be the way I am and who I am. In 1990, I'm coming back for more!"*

# Paul Noble

☐ TRACK & FIELD

☐ WELLINGTON, NEW ZEALAND

The setting would make any westerner feel right at home. Wellington, the capital city of New Zealand, has the look and feel of an American town. Near the center of town is a pedestrian mall. Trudging up a long flight of stairs off the mall, you will find a hair salon: a large, airy room with tall windows, two barber chairs and a small waiting area surrounded by thriving plants. An old fashioned ceiling fan and brass ornaments round out the decor.

Clients are greeted by Phillip or Paul. Phillip speaks rapidly with a thick British accent. Paul, of Maori descent, is quieter and chooses his words carefully. He is Phillip's apprentice and lover.

Paul Noble has a striking appearance. Dark features and a deep tan are accentuated by colorful tattoos running the length of each arm. His hair is cropped short, his clothes are loose fitting and comfortable. The noble heritage of his Maori blood is felt strongly as his 6' 2" frame towers over you. The Maoris are the aboriginal people of New Zealand, of Polynesian-Melanesian descent. He is the last person you would expect to find working as a hairdresser.

Paul is twenty years old. His trip to Gay Games II was his first journey off the islands of New Zealand. His eyes gave away an intense curiosity and anticipation when we met several months before the event. "I think of it being just like the Olympic Games or the Commonwealth Games (held recently in New Zealand). The only difference is that everyone will know how everyone else is—a sense of their sexuality. That's what I'm expecting to see, that's what I've heard about, all the hugging and openness. Plus there may be a majority of gay people there."

Paul's athletic background began at Rutherford School in Auckland, the largest city on the North Island. The English school system was well entrenched throughout New Zealand. Until recently, Maori's were beaten for speaking their native tongue at school. Paul played rugby and ran track for a number of years. He was a fast runner and represented both his school and local district in track meets.

Phillip explained to me the Maori concept of an extended family. At an early age, Maori children are reared by parents who are often not blood relatives. Whoever takes an interest in a baby can request permission to care for it. The sole exception is the eldest son, who is always brought up by grandparents.

Paul's family consisted of eleven children, all adopted except for his eldest brother Tom. After dropping out of school, Paul worked with his brother stringing power lines on the South Island for the state utility.

"I hadn't come out, and I didn't even accept that I was gay then. I'd had gay sexual experiences before that, but they were not very good. I was in a real confused state of mind—I didn't know what I was supposed to do. I wanted to be with another man but everyone else around me wanted to be with the opposite sex. So I made sure I kept it quiet. I had this horrible thought that I could keep it quiet for the rest of my life."

Moving out on his own, to Wellington, Paul found a number for the Gay Hotline under "G" in the phone book. Soon he had found a social outlet and more liberal attitudes. He met Phillip at a local sauna. They have been together for over two years and work side by side in the hairdressing trade.

For Gay Games II, Paul trained once again in track and field events. With Phillip and other New Zealand teammates watching, he won a gold medal in the shot-put event with a heave of 31.4 meters.

Once a lonely gay man in New Zealand, Paul Noble has now shared the thrill of this celebration with thousands of gay brothers and sisters. They represent for Paul the beginning of a new, more fulfilling extended family.

"I have gotten to know people from all over the world who came to the Gay Games to be part of this wonderful event. I feel enlightened towards the different culture in which you live," Paul wrote to me after the Games.

"With events like Gay Games II, the gay community will be strong enough to overcome the ill feelings towards all of us. The Games have made me feel much more positive towards myself and other people. They have made me proud to be the way I am and who I am. In 1990, I'm coming back for more!" ☐

The Story of Gay Games II

# Marathon

# PROFILES

*"The Gay Games ties into my own perception of being gay. Just to participate is an important statement of freedom and health. It shows the community at large that there are positive gay role models, as reflected in the men and women who compete in the Gay Games."*

# Dewey Ames

☐ MARATHON

☐ DETROIT, MICHIGAN

Northbound commuters pass the lone runner pacing through his morning ritual. It is early morning, the air is crisp and cold. Dewey Ames, with long easy strides, runs along Woodward Avenue in suburban Detroit. Like most long-distance runners, he trains year-round to keep in shape.

Dewey is a native of Michigan and works as a carpenter and painting contractor. His job allows him time to maintain his workout schedule, and on weekends he often competes in races over a variety of distances.

His running began, ironically, after an accident at work left him with several broken bones in his right foot. While laid up in the hospital, a friend brought him a few running and exercise books. His interest was piqued by Kenneth Cooper's *Aerobics*, and he slowly regained his strength by jogging. Within five months he competed in his first race of two miles, finishing third.

Dewey reached a milestone in his running career when he completed a Michigan marathon in 2:59:59. This qualified him for the Boston Marathon, just squeaking in under the three hour qualifying time. The Boston event is the granddaddy of all marathons, and has a mystique all its known. Dewey joined a huge field of runners for this race in 1979, crossing the finish line in a respectable 3:12:38.

An active participant in the gay community, Dewey has at times solicited sponsers to donate on a per-mile basis to "Wellness," a local AIDS support organization. A Maryland race raised $750 for this worthwhile cause.

In 1982 Dewey was startled to see a small write-up in the *Advocate* announcing Gay Games I. Later, while running through Palmer Park, a stranger stopped him and asked if he were planning to compete. Dewey eventually helped organize the Detroit team and made his way to San Francisco.

"Gay Games I was the most significant event of my life," Dewey recalls. Before his race, he met other gay athletes who tried to psyche each other out by reciting their best times. So he was surprised to find himself near the front of the pack of fifty runners as the marathon event, the first of Gay Games I, traced its way through Golden Gate Park and around Lake Merritt.

"We merged for a while with another shorter race, and those runners were cheering us on. It was quite incredible. Later, as I climbed the hill towards the Polo Field in Golden Gate Park, a cyclist told me I was in third place." This exhausted but triumphant runner from Michigan broke the tape at 2:58:13 to win the bronze medal.

Four years later, it looked as though financial problems would keep Dewey from running the marathon in the second Gay Games. He wrote to all his friends asking for help, and they responded just in time. Once again Dewey took pride in running alongside his gay brothers and sisters. He finished the marathon in 3:20:44, twenty-ninth overall.

"The Gay Games ties into my own perception of being gay. Just to participate is an important statement of freedom and health. It shows the community at large that there are positive gay role models, as reflected in the men and women who compete in the Gay Games." ☐

The Story of Gay Games II

PROFILES

*"I can't get over friends who just fall in and out of love. It's just not me. That may keep me lonely longer, but when I do finally find that person, it will last forever. I am loyal to people that I believe in."*

# Debbie Chaddock

TRACK, MARATHON □

SAN DIEGO, CALIFORNIA □

On the first day of competition at Gay Games II, Debbie Chaddock lost a tough race to Bridget Williams of Denver in the 10-K track event and finished second. All week she had a chance to think it over and rest up for the marathon, held on Sunday just before Closing Ceremonies.

At the marathon finish, cheers went up from the race monitors as the first female runner entered Kezar Stadium. Soon, the crowd joined in the applause. With her long steady pace, Debbie Chaddock eased across the finish line, cheered on by thousands. Her time was 3:09:15, good for a gold medal in the women's 18-29 age group. Only sixteen men finished ahead of her.

Debbie's first big thrill in sports was to finish third in the mile run in high school. Her time? A slow seven minutes.

Excellent coaching helped Debbie develop her natural running ability. She ran her first marathon at age twenty-three in the U.S. Olympic Sports Festival. She started last, then slowly picked up the pace. At the halfway point she was in second place, 3 minutes behind the leader. Then 2 1/2 minutes, then 2 minutes. With a mile to go, she passed the leader and won the race. At the time, she called it "the most memorable day of my life."

Gay Games II was a milestone in its own right. Debbie had trained hard with a group known as AIM, Athletes in Motion, which brought a strong group of athletes to the Games from San Diego. She volunteered as secretary and co-director of sports for AIM and helped to coach their running team. She is actively involved in the San Diego Frontrunners group as well.

Soft-spoken and demure, Debbie Chaddock seems remarkably well adjusted for a young woman of twenty-five. She is doing well in her profession, the graphic arts, and seems at ease in the gay community. During our interview she fielded my questions patiently, despite a nineteen-mile training run only hours before.

She told me that she has yet to settle down. "It takes me longer, I think, to warm up to people and feel for somebody. I can't get over friends who just fall in and out of love. It's just not me. That may keep me lonely longer, but when I do finally find that person, it will last forever. I am loyal to people that I believe in."

Debbie's running is in many ways a longstanding love relationship, one she has had since high school. "You hang around the running community, especially in San Diego, and they're supportive of women athletes, because we're different. We've overcome more."

Her community involvement includes the Greater San Diego Business Association, the Gay Academic Union and the Gay Youth Alliance.

"Through joining all those groups I developed a support system that was finally big enough and developed enough that I felt I could come out to my parents. If they totally rejected me, at least I had my second adopted family.

"I came out and found out how wonderful and special my parents are. I never would have known if I hadn't had the courage to come out to them, and being part of these groups helped me have that courage."

Debbie has found that athletic involvement within a social framework has taught her to embrace life as a gay person. Or, as she phrased it in our pre-Games interview (echoing the sentiments of Rita Mae Brown):

"It helps to know that you are not the only one in the world." □

A Sense of Pride:

The Story of Gay Games II

A Sense of Pride:

# Powerlifting

The Story of Gay Games II

## Profiles

*"I'm a very sensitive, caring, loving person, and I want that aspect of my personality to be just as apparent as my strength."*

# Shaun Wardinsky

POWERLIFTING □

PORTLAND, OREGON □

"I'm stronger than most men, and I literally have men walk out of the gym when I walk in, because of whatever sort of humility they may feel because I can outlift them.

"So I am careful who I lift with. I don't want to stigmatize the lesbian with a real strong *butch* dyke kind of image. I don't trust that the people at the gym are going to be able to see past that."

Meet Shaun Wardinsky, a very strong woman with a very warm heart. Her competition in the Gay Games, in the 67 kilo weight class (148 lbs), was tense and exciting. She told me that powerlifting involves psyching out the competition.

Shaun's first lift in the squat (taking a barbell off the rack, bending at the knees and straightening up again) was just over 300 pounds, higher than any opponent had tried. Down, then up. Two judges signaled a foul, meaning that her form was not correct.

On her second lift she chose to increase the weight slightly to 142.5 kilos (310 pounds). Down, then up. Once again, a judge nullified the effort.

Her third and last try, once again at 142.5 kilos, showed the determination of a true competitor. To the cheers of spectators in the crowded gym, the lift was successful. Shaun hefted a combined total of 392.5 kilos (865 lbs) in the squat, bench press and dead lift to win a gold medal in her weight class.

Serious weightlifters often train in old fashioned gyms, not the kind of place where you'd find Nautilus® machines or aerobics classes. Shaun's training routine includes workouts five days a week, exclusively with "free weights:" barbells not attached to any machinery.

Shaun met me in Portland with her lover Lynn. They both enjoy exercise, though in different sports. Lynn's passion is running. Her first road races gave her "a real sense of power, and a kind of oneness. The way your body moves in rhythm, you achieve a sense of well being where everything in that one instant is right."

Lynn is a teacher; Shaun works to prepare grants for non-profit organizations. Their schedules and interests are varied. "We both have been through changes in two years," Lynn relates. "Shaun and I have each worked hard to keep a sense of ourselves. It's a tough thing in a relationship, to be able to keep your boundaries and also become close."

Portland is a liberal city in many ways, but as lesbians, the pair is still somewhat closeted. Lynn worries about her teaching career in working with children. Shaun notes, "We can't walk down the street arm-in-arm. We're very careful. It's funny when we go on vacation when Lynn becomes so demonstrative to me. I'm taken aback ... I have to get used to it!"

Most people think of weight training as a macho sport, but macho is not a word that describes the warm, personable woman I interviewed. Shaun reflects on her life and her sport in a way that dispels any stereotypes:

"It has been a balancing act. There is a certain image of lesbians as being butch dykes, and I really resent that. I'm a very sensitive, caring, loving person too, and I want that aspect of my personality to be just as apparent as my strength.

"That's a lot of what the gay community has been responsible for, merging those two halves of myself and allowing me to be more of a total person." □

PHOTO GRAPHICS/DARLENE

The Story of Gay Games II

90 A Sense of Pride:

"In volleyball, you share such a deep feeling with your team. It's like a family . . . everybody's leading their own life off the court, yet you still share together."
—Roy Chalifour
Vancouver, BC, Canada

# Volleyball

92 A Sense of Pride:

# PROFILES

*"Participation has its own rewards. All of a sudden these people that have never played sport since they left school have got a chance. And nobody cares if they come in first or last."*

# Colin Fawcett

☐ VOLLEYBALL

☐ SYDNEY, AUSTRALIA

Colin Fawcett grew up in a small town outside Perth, Australia. He was a math and science whiz in school and kept to himself. He was not athletic nor did he join others to party. After six years of high school and half a year at the local university, he "realized there was more to life than sitting down reading a textbook."

Yes, and Colin also discovered he was gay. Like many Australians before him, he moved to Sydney to revel in its active gay lifestyle. At age twenty, Colin was ready to see some of the world.

Eight years later, he finds himself active in the gay community. His latest volunteer work is with the Sydney Gay Mardi Gras Association. "I really enjoy working with people, and I get personal satisfaction from events that are run well." Mardi Gras, held each year at the end of the summer, attracts gay people from all over Australia, as well as New Zealand and other countries.

Colin has enjoyed two long relationships since he moved to the city. His first lover was also named Colin ("unfortunate, that was"), with whom he "bought a house and lived happily ever after for two years."

He readily admits to his need for emotional involvement. "I quite enjoy knowing that there's somebody there to go home and have a chat with. You don't have to live together to get these types of benefits, but I do find it easier to actually share."

Athletics has never played a major role in his life, but Colin is nonetheless active in the Sydney Gay Sports Association and played volleyball on the Sydney team in Gay Games II. Tall and angular, he looks the part of a long-distance runner.

"I wouldn't say I was particularly good at any sport," he told me as we began the interview. Why, then, the involvement?" Trying to get these people out of the bars seven nights a week," he replies. "Participation has its own rewards. All of a sudden these people that have never played sport since they left school have got a chance. And nobody cares if they come in first or last.

"I feel that I must put something back into the community. It has supported me for a while. It's looked after me. It's provided a place for me to go and meet other people. I feel like I should do my bit to keep it going."

Colin describes his experience at Gay Games II as "the most inspiring thing that has happened to me. As we walked into Kezar Stadium, people cheered and shouted not because you were a great sportsman, but because you were a gay sportsman. There was an overwhelming feeling of togetherness and pride.

"If you described them as the 'friendly games,' it would be an understatement. In one week, this event united gay men and women from all over the world into one big family. Our next family reunion is in Vancouver in 1990. I can hardly wait!" ☐

JOHN JENNER

## Profiles

*"The Games were awesome!"*

# Kris Medinger

VOLLEYBALL COACH □

BOSTON, MASSACHUSETTS □

Looking butch in a short-cropped haircut and shorts, Kris Medinger pulled up on roller skates for our interview in Boston. We're not talking about a short trip in the neighborhood here. This was halfway across town, about 20 minutes by car!

Kris is outspoken and outrageous. Surprisingly, she was at first reluctant to have her profile in a book on the Gay Games. "Finally, somebody said to me, 'Just think. In 200 years, some budding young lesbian will pick up this book and see a hot dyke, and they'll be all set.' So I figured if you're going to come out, you might as well go out all the way."

At 30, Kris is the coach for men's volleyball in Boston. Yes, she's the boss for two teams that competed in Gay Games II, Men's B Division. The Boston group (their first team) finished fifth overall in the tournament, a respectable showing in a field of twenty.

Kris feels natural about the interplay with gay men: "It's no different than coaching women. I do miss the kind of companionship that happens when you're the same sex and you go into the locker room and joke around with your team. But I feel like men get their periods too!"

She admits that the first few weeks of coaching were stressful. "I choked down and started with an aggressive approach, took them from square one and tried to ignore the fact that these were 6' 4" men with moustaches.

"I had a lot of generic fears about men because I didn't know any closely. I've realized how much I love men and that a lot of things I was afraid of, I'm not afraid of anymore."

And relationships with women? It would be hard for someone to find a niche in her life right now. Between coaching and part-time jobs, Kris' schedule is hectic. She is also taking courses at the University of Massachusettes needed to enter chiropractic school.

Kris majored in health and physical education at Virginia Commonwealth University. Her first encounter with another lesbian occurred freshman year: "I knew if I paid her a lot of attention and touched her it was OK, so there was subconscious there. I had agreed to sleep over. We were sitting in bed when she hooked my leg—and I've tried this with other women to figure out how she did it—then lifted it somehow so I would have to roll over right into her arms."

Kris played both basketball and volleyball in college and learned coaching techniques. After graduation, she moved first to Provincetown and then to Boston. For two years, she coached the Stonehill College women's volleyball team. With her guidance, Stonehill went from a record of 1-14 to 5-10 in Kris' first year, then 15-8 the following season.

During a game, Kris is a picture of concentration. She kneels courtside, signalling her team, playing each point as intensely as the men she coaches. She moves with the ball, showing a look of anticipation before the spike, an expression of pain if an opportunity is blown.

"I like volleyball because you don't touch anyone other than your own teammates. I don't like contact. I find it real offensive when you are guarding your spot on the bag in softball and people just mow you over, a real butch thing to do.

"I think volleyball's a real clean kill. It is very dignified. You line up beforehand, nod to your teammates, go out on the court and whomp 'em with the ball. I also like it because it's a true team sport. You rarely have one person singled out as a star."

In August 1986, Kris and 'her men' headed to San Francisco for Gay Games II. "This is a time," she remarked, "for people who have never competed in their lives, who have had nothing to do with athletics, to find out how exciting it is to compete against people from all over the world. I have done that, on a very minimal college level, but this seems like it couldn't be more positive.

"The Games were awesome!" □

## PROFILES

*"I like to be on stage, performing."*

# Richard Dopson

☐ VOLLEYBALL

☐ VANCOUVER, BC, CANADA

In 1982, the young Vancouver volleyball team headed to Denver with cheerful abandon, knowing little of what to expect when they arrived. They were new to the sport, and the sport was new on the Vancouver gay scene. The trip took twenty-eight hours in a Chevy van. Nine players, who had practiced for weeks before, became a closer-knit group on that trip. Richard Dobson recalls:

"Three of us fit in the cab. We just talked for hours, about our lives and our loves. It felt like we really got to know one another, and a kinship developed."

The team finished ninth in the tournament, winners of the consolation round. For Richard, it was the genesis of his interest in organized sport for the gay and lesbian community.

Later that year they traveled to the first Gay Games. The Vancouver team returned home glowing with enthusiasm over their week in San Francisco.

"It was such an emotional high for the Closing Ceremonies," Richard recalls. "The crowd was screaming and everybody was just vibrating with excitement. We came to the event not knowing what to expect and were greeted by thousands—what a rush!"

In Vancouver, as in other cities, Gay Games I provided the spark for local athletes to organize their own leagues and organizations. Richard and others formed the Metropolitan Vancouver Arts & Athletics Association (MVAAA).

This is pretty heady stuff for a guy from the plains of Canada, Winnipeg to be exact. "It's a small town in many ways," Richard notes, "especially in their attitudes. The move to Vancouver was a calculated and important move for me. I wanted to integrate my personal and social life, so I could live and work in the city and also have a gay lifestyle."

He is close to his mother Mary, who has also moved to Vancouver. She accepts his lifestyle without question—"she comes to every party I have"—and appreciates his circle of friends.

Richard sees athletics as a way of helping many in the gay community "come out to themselves and come out to other people—significant others—because they have a big support group. It gives them a base to make a change in their life."

Always on the move, rarely at home, Richard Dobson is a whirlwind of energy. In prior years he worked with four semi-professional theater groups. Even now he recognizes this as part of his motivation, saying simply: "I like to be on stage, performing."

Richard will get his chance in 1990. Vancouver's bid for Gay Games III was accepted and the wheels are already in motion. He and others from his committee were heard saying, "We hope to do as well as you have, though I don't know how we could outdo this week you have put together."

And yet, it will not matter how many athletes join the fun in 1990, nor how many sports are included, nor how glitzy the Ceremonies turn out to be. What is important is the continuation of the dream.

Knowing Richard, Gay Games III will be Vancouver's own, the sum total of their unique collective vision, borne of their love for and involvement in the gay community. ☐

The Story of Gay Games II

# PROFILES

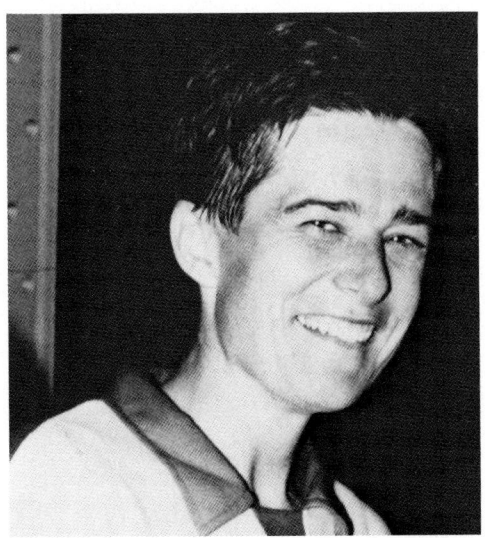

*"I honestly believe that what I saw in San Francisco was a first ... the first time I'd seen the kind of international sporting event that also catered to people's need to come together and play for fun. That is something that competitive sports lost a long time ago."*

# Betty Baxter

☐ VOLLEYBALL

☐ VANCOUVER, BC, CANADA

Few of us can boast of competing against world class athletes in our sport. Fewer still have felt the range of emotions that Betty Baxter has seen in her athletic career. For Betty, the peak experience came while training for the 1976 Olympics with the Canadian women's volleyball team:

"We were playing the Japanese team, the top women's team anywhere. I was one of our power hitters, and scored a direct point against their best player. That moment was special because it gave me a sense of personal achievement and pride in beating somebody that was the best in the world. I remember that one-on-one situation, and feeling, 'This is what it's been about all this time.'"

Betty's eyes betray her boundless energy and intensity. They sparkle with life and demand your attention. Since age 19, she is a woman who has set out to make her mark on Canadian sports.

The 1976 Summer Games, held in Montreal, saw a resurgence of athletic fervor in her country. The Canadian women's volleyball team was excellent that year. Betty, as team captain, led her team through the preliminary rounds. In their match against Peru, where they were favored, the Canadians let the final game slip away 15-12. Betty has played the last point over again and again in her mind.

"The most emotional experience, the one that left the deepest mark in my heart, was losing the final point that knocked us out of the medal round in the Olympic Games. It was a ball I could have played. It came to my position and there was so much stress, so much pressure on us. I'll remember that second for the rest of my life."

After the Olympics, she became the first Canadian and the first woman ever to coach their national team. Two years later, amidst rumors that she was a lesbian, Betty was suddenly fired. "Something critical in my life was taken away," she recalls. "I had lots of anger toward the straight sports system because of that. It has taken me four years to feel good about going back into volleyball."

Betty cites Gay Games I as a catalyst that helped her slowly rebuild her confidence and self-respect. She visited San Francisco as a spectator in 1982 and watched her lover Anita compete in soccer. "For me to come out of the straight sport world which had just walked over me for six months, and then to see the Gay Games was an exhilarating event. It was healthy and therapeutic. First I was shafted for my sexuality, then found a whole city celebrating it!"

Her banishment from coaching left Betty with a bitter taste for the system that she once trusted, a system into which she had poured years of her life. She reflects on women in sports:

"I came out in a kind of jock circle, always behind closed doors. There was a large community of us, but not in any public way. At the time I was fired, I knew hundreds of lesbians across Canada, none of whom would ever say it in public. They wouldn't even say the word 'lesbian.'

"Even now, I know scores of women who will sit around a dinner party with four or five of their closest friends, their partners are there, and they never acknowledge that anyone at the table is sexually attached to anyone else. Ever."

Betty maintains a strong commitment to sports. She serves on the organizing committee that will host Gay Games III in Vancouver in 1990, and recently returned to coaching (this time for kids age 15-19). She also helped to organize the Canadian Association for the Advancement of Women in Sports. Their goal: to help women move up the ranks in the male-dominated coaching profession.

At Gay Games II, she led her Vancouver team to the gold medal in women's volleyball. The final match against Berkeley was dramatic. In the third and deciding game, Betty spiked the winning ball and Vancouver won, 15-11 ... perhaps an echo of that last point she had replayed so often since the '76 Olympics.

"I honestly believe that what I saw in San Francisco was a first, and I've been involved in sports for 20 years. It was the first time I'd seen the kind of international sporting event that also catered to people's need to come together and play for fun. That is something that competitive sports lost a long time ago." ☐

The Story of Gay Games II

## Profiles

*"I think there is some kind of change that takes place emotionally when you're exercising or stretching."*

# Yolanda Retter

RACQUETBALL ☐

LOS ANGELES, CALIFORNIA ☐

The first of Yolanda Retter's two business cards reads: INFORMATION BROKER, a job that entails locating information in books, journals, computers and people. When we met she was busy entering keywords for articles on Latino issues into a personal computer.

In her apartment, books of all kinds are stacked to the ceiling—books on Latin America, airplane mechanics, martial arts, psychology and a variety of other subjects. Yolanda has spent years reading and learning. At thirty-eight, she is a woman with many interests and skills.

Her other business card reads: ITINERANT COMMUNITY WORKER. "My commitment is to lesbian/gay and women's issues in general, and women of color in particular. I lend a hand to projects as they come up. This has taken the form of helping to organize conferences and marches, managing the security for several street fairs, conducting workshops on controversial topics, helping to start the L. A. Women's Yellow Pages and so forth."

Yolanda's life has been filled with twists and turns. She was born in Connecticut. At age four, she moved with her family to El Salvador ("before anyone knew where it was") and lived there for eight years. In her early teens, she moved back to Connecticut, then to California to attend college. She has lived there ever since.

Along the way, Yolanda learned the art of cabinet building and aircraft mechanics. She once served as Director of a Rape Hotline. With a Masters degree in Library Science, she is now studying for a second Masters (in Social Work) at UCLA.

She presently works at Connexxus, a local Women's center in Los Angeles. There, she serves an Administrative Intern and Coordinator of the Latina Outreach Program. "I see my commitment to women as a way to support the powerful promise women have for improving conditions on the planet."

When Yolanda counsels individuals, she encourages them to integrate exercise and sport into their therapy. "For example, I have gone with a person out to a track. As we talk, we walk and run, and then talk some more. Exercising opens the body, opens the psyche up for healing and change."

Yolanda has been playing racquetball for four years. "I think of it as a movement mediation, similar to a martial art. It teaches me on a physical, emotional, mental and spiritual level."

Although she lost in the first round at Gay Games II, she is glad that she made the effort to join other athletes. "I felt a sense of responsibility in a positive way to participate, to contribute to the energy and the spirit of the Games." She plans to play in the 1988 Gay Games in Vancouver, British Columbia. ☐

*(Left) A son watches his mother compete from the gallery.*

# Racquetball

ROY COE

MICK HICKS

The Story of Gay Games II

"Swimming is a lonely sport ... I do a lot of thinking, putting things in perspective. When you're swimming laps there is not much else you can do. But I get off on the exercise. 'Hitting the wall' really gets to me. After 1,000 yards, I feel like I could swim all day. When you hit the wall, you cross into the ozone where there's no pain. I don't feel it anymore."
—Bruce Erickson (below)
Seattle, Washington

# Swimming

102  A Sense of Pride:

# PROFILES

*"Being gay is only part of what we are. We're not defined just in terms of our sexual orientation. A lot of people are working to develop diversity in the gay community. The Gay Games is one way of doing just that."*

# Rick Peterson

☐ SWIMMING

☐ SEATTLE, WASHINGTON

The spirited team from Seattle, Washington had a logo, a slogan—*The Gay and Lesbian Varsity*—and a few PR gimmicks up their sleeve. As athletes gathered for Closing Ceremonies at Gay Games II, a huge banner rose into the sky. Spelled out in white and green balloons (their team colors) was their rallying cry, **TEAM SEATTLE**.

There is little doubt that Rick Peterson, an ad agency copywriter, had a hand in the hoopla. One of his current clients is a major class-eight truck manufacturer. "So," he says with a grin, "here you've got a gay male who is putting all the words into one of the butchest companies in North America!"

Rick is a competitive swimmer. He trained voraciously for years and competed through college on an athletic scholarship. Eventually, the fun was gone. He describes it as "total burnout."

Three years ago he began to swim again and encouraged others to take up the sport. On his lunch break, he usually swims about 2000 yards. After a warmup he works on interval training, a predetermined number of yards with rest time factored in.

"The training helps you understand what pacing is all about. When you go into a race you have to know what it feels like to go fast. You have to understand what it feels like to work. You have to be comfortable with both and not be unwilling to push yourself. It is also a great way to get an aerobic workout."

As co-chairperson, Rick is one of the prime movers behind Team Seattle. This was tough on his relationship of twelve years with his lover David. David's job schedule, working at Seattle Center, is usually at odds with Rick's 9 to 5. Although it's "a nightmare" to find quality time together, their relationship remains strong.

The two own a house in suburban Seattle, a very American setting amidst a row of family dwellings. As you drive up, it is hard to pick out their home from the others. The furnishings are personalized and comfortable. An enthusiastic dog named Mouse greeted me at the door.

Rick Peterson is never content, however, to blend in with his surroundings. He has worked with the Northwest AIDS Foundation as a board member in the movement to educate and motivate the community towards safe sex. The campaign he worked on was called "Choose Life."

To Rick, the issue was not the safe sex guidelines themselves but the motivation to change behavior: the process of translating knowledge into practice.

"A lot of people are fatalistic about AIDS. What we wanted to say is that by doing certain things, you *can* take control of your life. As gay people we should be living fuller lives, reaching out and making the most of everything in our lives, not just sex." Rick views athletics as one way for these alternatives to develop. Team Seattle encouraged both competitive and recreational athletes to participate.

"On an emotional level, you find very different motivational factors for each person. This shows that there is a lot more to Gay Games II than just the competition. It's a real celebration of our community which goes beyond whoever wins a particular event, or who comes in tenth.

"Being gay is only part of what we are. We're not defined just in terms of our sexual orientation. A lot of people are working to develop diversity in the gay community. The Games are one way of doing just that."

By coincidence, Rick bumped into Richard Hunter (see Richard's profile) on the BART subway platform at 24th and Mission in San Francisco. They were both headed to Laney College in Oakland for the first day of swimming competition at Gay Games II. The meeting was friendly but ironic since the two were to compete head to head all week long.

Rick Peterson took home seven medals from the Games, including golds in the 50, 200 and 500 yard freestyle events. ☐

The Story of Gay Games II

## Profiles

*"We can be above the negative things that have always ruled and dominated us in the past."*

# Mark Wussler

SWIMMING □

SAN DIEGO, CALIFORNIA □

"We rose above ourselves. I am so proud of our team and the people I helped coach. My own performance I pretty much expected, but everyone did so well and knocked seconds off their times."

Here is a man who is always in motion. Even when you sit down to talk, there is something in his body language that tells you that he rarely sits still. Sentences flow together and his train of thought races ahead of the conversation.

Here is Mark Wussler: someone who twisted many arms to convince others to participate in Gay Games II. Now, "all of them are so greatful and have thanked me. I kept true to the promise I made after the last Games, that I would see as many people here as possible enjoying the same feeling I had. Our community needs that so much."

Mark worked with AIM, Athletes In Motion, the San Diego group that sponsored local athletes attending Gay Games II. As a coach, he helped organize the San Diego swimming team.

His own athletic performance peaked at just the right moment, perfectly aligned with his enthusiasm for the Gay Games. At the Laney College swimming competition, Mark knocked *40 seconds* off his best time in his strongest event, the 1650 meter freestyle (1 mile). This earned him a gold medal in his age group, and he went home with seven other medals as well.

At 30 years old, Mark swam a personal best in every event he entered, faster than times achieved in high school or college.

He competed for Tucson, Arizona at Gay Games I in 1982, and moved to San Diego two years later. Athletics provides a social network that continues year round. Mark enjoys the wide variety of outdoor exercise afforded by the southwest's mild climate. Hiking and camping are two of his favorites. On a sunny day, he is often found at Black's Beach—and leaves his swim suit behind.

Just where does all this energy come from?

"I want to be able to bottle it and sell it, because so many people seem to want it. But believe me, it gets me in as much trouble as it does anything else. [I believe him!] I got my share of smacks with a ruler from the nuns in grade school."

Mark looks forward to an AIDS fundraiser in January of 1987, a half-marathon swim (3.1 miles). "There is a lot of money being spent on the Gay Games, on what could be viewed as a real selfish venture. You know, patting ourselves on the back and having our own little Games. To those people, I want to be able to say, 'We are doing our part, we're doing things for the community too.'"

The payoff for Mark comes when he sparks the enthusiasm of others and gets them moving together. By the end of four days of grueling competition in San Francisco, swim teams from the west coast had agreed to form a league and hold regional meets. The first? To be held in San Diego, of course.

"For me the Games are a realization that we can, as a community, be above our circumstances. We can be above what we're resigning ourselves to. We *have* to do that if we're going to survive. We must realize that we don't have to make the same mistakes we've made before.

"Competitiveness, negativity, beating the other person—the flag waving, the gold medal counting, all that kind of stuff—the Games are above it. You can have 3500 people get together, and those people leave with the sense that something special and wonderful can happen, and we will survive.

"We can be above those kinds of negative things that have always ruled and dominated us in the past." □

A Sense of Pride:

# PROFILES

*"To lose is not to fail: To fail is not to have tried at all."*

# Richard Hunter

☐ SWIMMING

☐ NEWHALL, CALIFORNIA

To reach Newhall, you drive north from Los Angeles on Interstate 5. The road winds over a pass through the Angeles National Forest, coiling around hills, dry and brown in the summer. Beyond the pass lies a slice of suburbia carved into the Santa Clarida Valley. Richard Hunter lives and works here, far from the thriving gay community in Los Angeles.

He moved to Newhall from the LA basin to be closer to the stables where he rides his horse preparing for competition. The races are long and grueling—50 or 100 miles in length. It is a sport he loves and can enjoy only in a country setting.

Richard is well known for his swimming exploits in Gay Games I. He won ten gold and two silver medals, and bettered three of his lifetime personal records. The picture on the cover of this book shows a moment of exultation from 1982. He recalls the deafening support from crowds at the swimming competition:

"I never had an audience that was so proud of me and made me feel so proud of what I was representing, what I was doing. They were living this experience through me. I never felt such energy to perform. I get chills and tears when I think about it."

As the second Games approached, Richard felt the pressure of his past performance from teammates. "Do it again," they would say. "LA's depending on you." He knew the competition would be rougher, and injuries hampered his training.

His swimming career began at age eleven and peaked at the high school level when he won first place in the Southern California Interscholastic Federation in the 50 and 100 yard freestyle events.

Then Richard attended UCLA. As a sprinter on the swim team, he burned out on the long workouts demanded at the collegiate level. It is a state of mind that many swimmers reach.

After college, Richard embarked on a brief modeling career in Europe, then returned to LA to work in real estate. When the bottom dropped out of the market he took work with the post office, and he's now a letter carrier in Newhall.

He describes his competitive instincts in personal terms: "In all honesty, the person I'm most afraid of is myself. You can win with a lousy time, and it doesn't mean anything. But I can also get a fifth place doing my best time. Then I know that I've trained well and I'm at my peak. That's what means most to me."

Overcoming the fear of failure is a key element for many athletes who enter the Gay Games. The mentality of our age eulogizes winners and ignores those who fall behind. Richard's motto: "To lose is not to fail: To fail is not to have tried at all."

Richard balances his need for privacy—the long distance horseback rides alone, a quiet life in Newhall and a personal training ritual—with the need for group support and acknowledgment.

"When I was competing in Gay Games I, I looked up at that grandstand with all those people, and it was like I was doing it for everybody there. It wasn't just for me anymore. I was giving again. I was doing it for the gay community. It becomes meaningful. It's important for me to feel that I am sharing and doing something for others."

Richard Hunter and Rick Peterson dueled in the freestyle events throughout the spirited swimming competition of Gay Games II. Richard swam with the Los Angeles team and came home with nine medals, including a gold in the 50 yard breaststroke. He also won a gold medal swimming for an LA relay team, the men and women's mixed medley. ☐

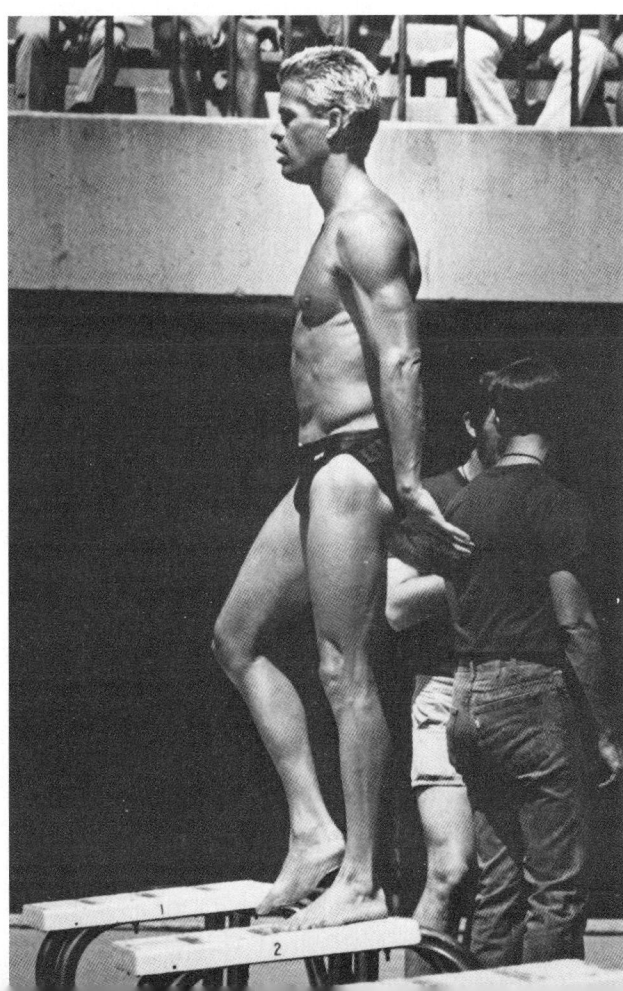

The Story of Gay Games II

# PROFILES

*"Comaraderie is something that I never expected to see as a gay person, and now I am seeing it."*

# Craig Mallery

☐ SWIMMING

☐ BOSTON, MASSACHUSETTS

A month before Gay Games II, I told Craig Mallery that he would find many swimmers there who were very competitive. Without skipping a beat, he replied "but are they fast?"

So it goes in the sport of swimming, where races are measured in tenths and hundredths of a second. Craig has thrived for years in this competitive atmosphere. He has been swimming since the age of nine. His specialty is the freestyle and he is an extremely fast sprinter.

In the finals for the 50 yard freestyle at Gay Games II, Craig set a Pacific Coast Masters record with a time of 21.81 seconds. All told, he went home with five gold medals, one for each event he entered.

Craig, age twenty-three, was raised in Woodland, California, near Sacramento. He moved to Boston for school and has found New England to be a much less intense sports environment than the west coast. "People don't have a swimming mentality here," he notes with a smile, "they have a hockey mentality."

Craig admits that he grew up as "a loner of sorts." It was hard to make close friends because he moved among three different high school swim programs. His family situation was not a happy one and his parents have separated. Consequently, swimming served as Craig's primary focus for a long time. The sport and its demanding training schedule gave him a sense of continuity in life, along with rewards for achievement.

It was not until college that Craig first explored his sexuality. His first lover, David, was also an athlete. They built their relationship while living in the athletic dorm at Boston University, surrounded by football, hockey and basketball players.

The dorm and the prevailing "jock mentality" of its residents was intimidating. Craig was at first defensive and shy, but finally learned to relax and accept the fact that he was gay. Ultimately, he found that other athletes could accept it as well.

"Swimming is something that has been great for my self-esteem. I think it has also helped me in dealing with being gay. I grew up in a small town, and a gay person to someone in a small town is a very flamboyant, effeminate figure. I discovered from the closest source I know—me—that his doesn't have to be true."

Craig is studying for a degree in sports psychology at Boston University. He hopes to apply his competitive experience to help other athletes develop their potential. His dream is to become a sports psychologist for the U. S. Olympic Team.

Prior to Gay Games II, Craig helped coach other gay swimmers in Boston. This forced him to adjust his style. "I think I come across as pushy, and these guys weren't in it to be pushed. They were there to have fun, and that's great. But it has taken me a while to understand that not everyone is out for blood and guts."

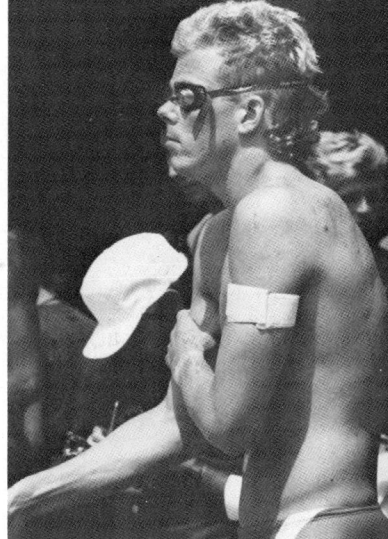

The interaction with other gay athletes is a new experience, and offers a different way of relating to peers outside the confines of a swimming pool.

"Comaraderie is something that I never expected to see as a gay person, and now I am seeing it. To me, that is very important. Knowing myself, I could probably go through life being gay and not develop a network of gay friends. That has been a process I've avoided. But now it feels great. Something like the Gay Games provides an ideal opportunity for me."

The Story of Gay Games II

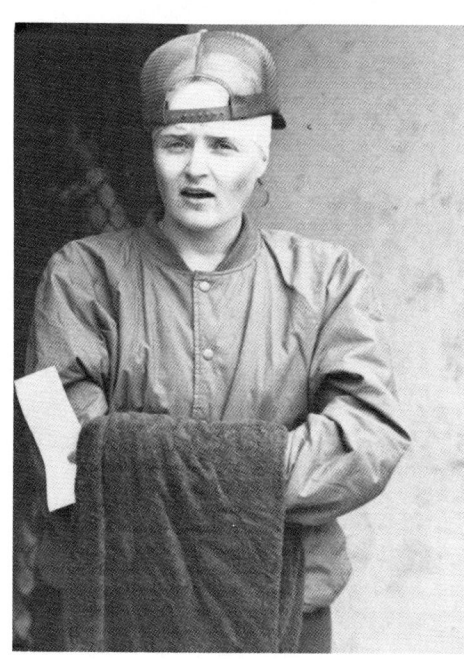

ROY COE

# PROFILES

*"This is a job where you get immediate feedback. The crowd will let me know if I did a good job."*

Katherine and her lover Darien are shown at left.

# Katherine Krebs

☐ DIRECTOR OF OPENING & CLOSING CEREMONIES

☐ SAN FRANCISCO, CALIFORNIA

"I've always wanted to be in the Olympics. I like all the pageantry and the color and the nations. I like to feel that championship feeling."

Katherine Krebs works in convention management. Her first event was in 1976 at the New Orleans Superdome. "It was set up for basketball. During noon hour I would go out to center court and shoot baskets. It was great fun just to be in the center of the Superdome and imagine myself performing in front of thousands of people."

Katherine shares a home in the district known as Noe Valley with her lover Darien. In the back of the house, past an office and through the kitchen, is an airy living and dining space that opens up to the back yard. Stacks of paper and files are a testimony of work done at the dining room table.

Our interview was held ten days before Opening Ceremonies for Gay Games II. Katherine was director of this elaborate event. I found her busy poring over endless last minute details.

"I know that show inside out and out, second by second. We agonized over it for months. When it finally begins I'll probably stand there and cry. All the people coming from little towns all around the world—places you've never heard of—people who care enough to come thousands of miles to participate in this event.

"I wish I could read the thoughts of all the people who are going to be there, to know how they feel and to know if I feel is what they feel."

Opening Ceremonies began with a flourish at 1:00 PM on the dot, with the introduction of Rita Mae Brown as MC. Bands played, dancers danced and baton twirlers twirled. Finally came the moment that Katherine had played out in her imagination a hundred times—the parade of athletes from around the world. Gay Games II was underway!

Behind the scenes her lover Darien worked as associate producer. It was an unusual partnership and at times stressful. They found it hard hard to draw the lines of authority. But the relationship survived the Games, a tribute to their love and commitment.

Katherine is sincere when she says, "It's always been the most important thing for me to be in a loving, committed relationship. Number two has been to have a home and number three has been to have a job that I like. For the first time in my life, I have all three." She has worked hard for it.

In 1982, at the first Gay Games, Katherine won the first of four medals early in the swimming competition. "Darien was so proud of me that she bought a *humongous* bouquet of red roses tied with a lavender ribbon. When I went up on the victory stand, she rushed out from the crowd with this fabulous bouquet and I was overwhelmed. The crowd went wild!"

After Gay Games I, Katherine pursued Tom Waddell with phone calls and letters in order to get involved again the second time around. She wanted to see to it that the second Gay Games would be filled with many of those same special moments.

In addition to her committee duties, Katherine found time to compete in Gay Games II, winning seven medals in swimming. She successfully defended her '82 gold medal in the 50 yard backstroke. Katherine and Darien also hosted Annie Boiteux, a member of the French women's volleyball team, and her lover Christiane during the week.

Opening and Closing Ceremonies, where tears flowed freely, were events that will be remembered for years. They were the product of careful planning, Katherine's devotion (she even helped paint) and the imagination of countless volunteers.

"The biggest pleasure I get out of my work is to have things go perfectly, to plan well in advance and then watch the whole thing unfold. This is a job where you get immediate feedback. The crowd will let me know if I did a good job."

Thousands of spectators, athletes and volunteers shared the same feelings, and they let Katherine know: Opening and Closing Ceremonies were simply fabulous! ☐

The Story of Gay Games II

# Tennis

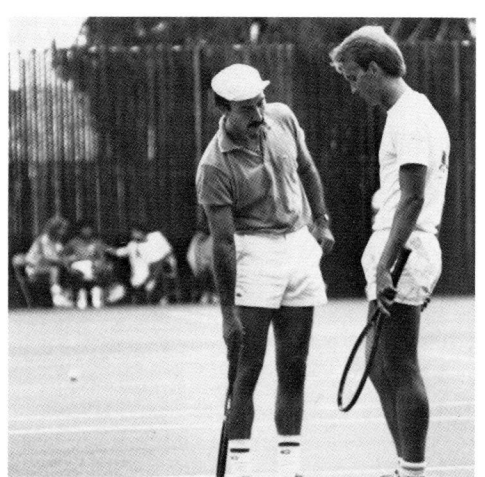

*"When I was younger, I was terribly uncoordinated. Good grades were no problem, but sports were more important with your peers. I always wanted to play, to be good, but I never was. Now I've discovered that I'm a pretty good athlete. I finally grew into it."*
—Doug Ford
San Diego, California

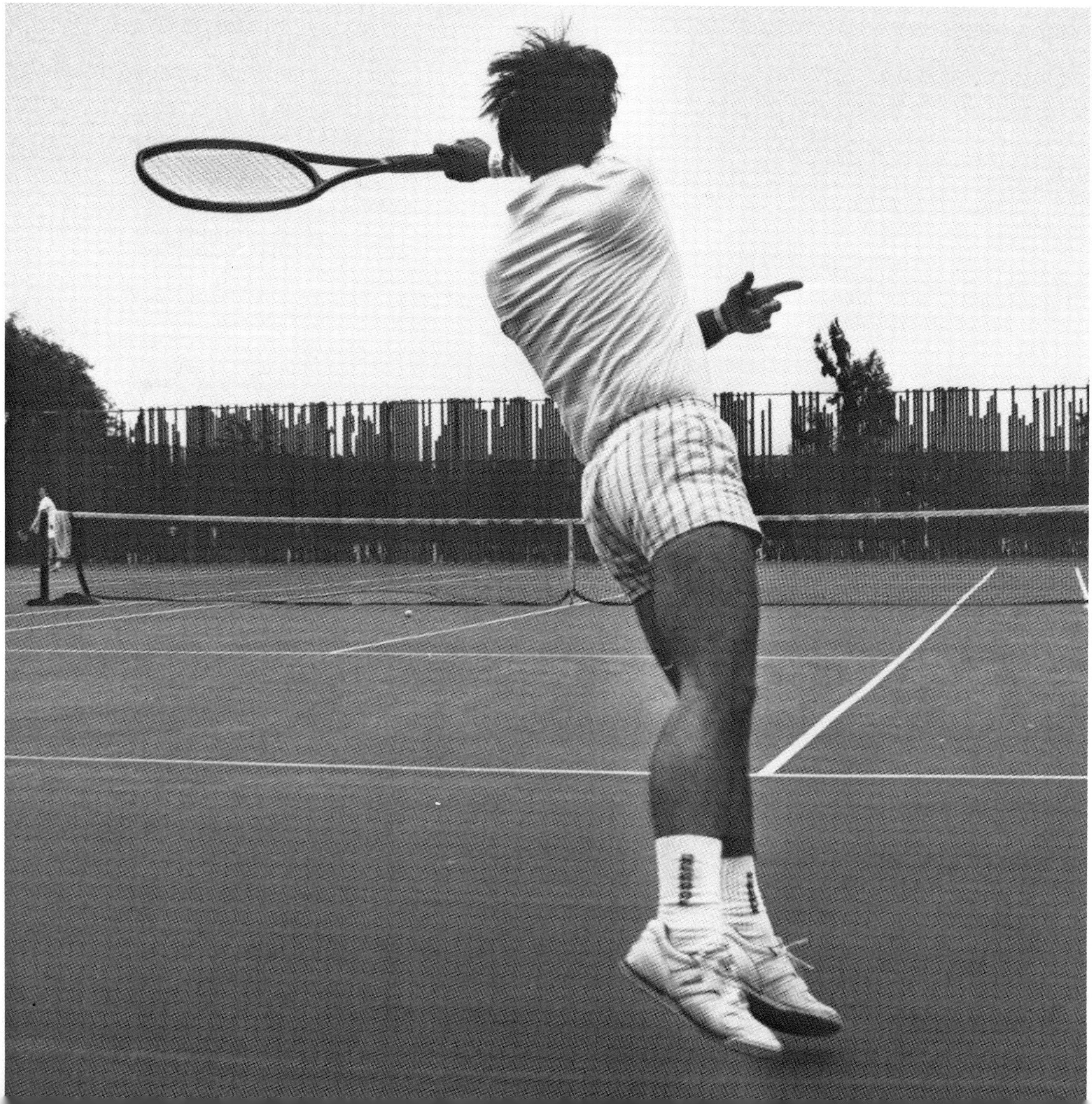

PATSY LYNCH

# PROFILES

*"For me, tennis is really a mixture of art and sport. And it leans towards art ..."*

# Bob Schulte

☐ TENNIS

☐ WASHINGTON, DC

Bob Schulte packed his bags to leave Iowa and his family behind, and headed for Washington, DC. "At the train station, a little depot, my parents were there crying, waving goodbye to their son as they put him on the train going to the big city with two suitcases ... it's so cliché, but that's exactly what happened."

He adds with a smile, half joking, "I'd be mortified if this came out in the interview!"

Bob's childhood days growing up in a small town is a classic American story line. Everyone in Mediapolis, Iowa (halfway between Wapello and Burlington) went to the same grammar school and high school. His father was the town banker. He has forty first cousins and is one of six children in "a large extended family."

College, an hour and a half away, was the first break from this routine. "My dormitory had more people in it than my home town did, so that was a bit of a shock! I went to college for theater and got a degree in directing. This was real different from what they normally do in Iowa."

Upon graduation, he was offered a theater job in Washington, DC. It was the right place for a country boy to feel OK about being gay ... which he took care of in just five days! His past and present were "night and day." He recalls: "All my relationships were new, so having come out the first week, I didn't have to go back and retrace many steps."

At thirty, Bob has played tennis for several years but only practiced seriously in the recent past. As a personal challenge, he entered the annual DC Sports Tournament (a local gay league). He shocked the competition, and himself, by taking home the trophy for first place.

For Bob, tennis gives reign to an alter-ego, one which is satisfied by fierce competition. "The court allows my feelings of aggression to be expressed. It's a place where it's socially acceptable to want to kill the other person, right? Well, I've learned to own up to some of these feelings off the court too, and found ways to deal with them. Tennis has been a helpful bridge to finding out more about myself."

A knee injury nearly kept Bob away from Gay Games II. He decided to enter anyway, knowing that he was not in top condition. He was defeated in the first round by Scott Williford of San Diego (see Scott's Profile).

"I had hoped to fare better in my match," Bob admits, "but losing is an experience too. Life doesn't end because you're not at your best. I took to heart the Gay Games theme that participation itself was worthwhile. I enjoyed the week and the people I met ... and being a part of history!"

Social work is Bob's career goal, a new direction after managing his own housekeeping business. After Gay Games II, he returned to school to work for a Masters in Social Work. "To really understand the stresses and challenges of others," he notes, "you have to experience some of them yourself."

A demon on the tennis court, a charmer in person, Bob Schulte offers many contrasts to those who know him: at once gentle and unassuming, yet fiercely competitive. Beneath it all is the subtle influence of his days in theater and drama.

"For me, tennis is really a mixture of art and sport. And it leans towards art because of the strategy, the shots and the gracefulness of playing it. If you slowed tennis down, if you see it in slow motion, it's almost ballet. ☐

The Story of Gay Games II

## PROFILES

*"We have a very good understanding of each other. We each recognize that there are both 'adult' and 'child' elements in our personalities. It's okay to be silly and you don't always need to be grown up. There's a time and place for all of it."*

# Jeff Greene & Ray Geerlof

WRESTLING □

LOS ANGELES, CALIFORNIA □

Jeff and Ray's apartment reflects their playful spirit. An indoor basketball hoop hangs from one wall. Teddy bears, an entire menagerie, peer out from one corner of the living room: meet Mr. Fudge, Percy and Coco, Sheldon and Shaggy, Spunky and Woggles, Puppy and Bamboo, Oscar and McDuff, Topsie, Tootie, Flopsie and Boo Boo. Are these guys serious? "Sometimes I think we're little kids in adult bodies," Ray admits.

"I think we'd both like to remain boys and play Monopoly and not have to work," Jeff adds. "In our old apartment, we would throw each other around, just playing, and we'd put holes in the walls without even trying!"

Both Ray and Jeff wrestle with the Los Angeles team. Ray attends college in New York City during the school year. Jeff lives and works year-round in Los Angeles as a promoter of large-scale events.

Ray is twenty-one and studies athletic administration. He learned to wrestle in high school and plays competitive basketball as well. While living with his family two years ago, he spotted Jeff walking down the street and asked him if *he* knew how to wrestle. They have been together ever since.

Jeff, age twenty-six, met Ray in New Jersey, then both men moved to Los Angeles. Now, for nearly seven months out of the year, Ray and Jeff are separated when Ray goes back East to school.

"The first Saturday night he was gone," Jeff recalls, "I had gone out with friends. When I came home, about 5:30 in the morning, I went to the bedroom and lay down. As I realized for the first time that he wasn't going to be there, I called him up—"

"And we're still paying off the phone bill!" Ray adds. "I'm glad I have this relationship rather than being on my own right now. Before we met, I had never been to a bar or gotten involved in the gay world. Now that I am, I enjoy it.

"But when I'm out with friends back in New York, I'll turn around to look for him at the pinball machine and he won't be there. Naturally all my friends know Jeffrey already, though they haven't met him, because I talk about him all the time."

One day in April 1986 Ray came home from work to find Jeff dressed in his Los Angeles team uniform, practicing his wave to the crowd at Opening Ceremonies. He stood up on the bed and leaned over in mock ceremony to receive his medal. "It was so funny. He just put on a tape, got changed and marched around the apartment."

They found the turnout of wrestlers at the Games a bit disappointing, though this meant that everyone had a better shot at a medal. Jeff and Ray both took golds in their respective age groups and weight class. There were only three heavyweight wrestlers entered, all different ages, so Ray and Jeff wrestled an exhibition match (Ray won).

The Los Angeles wrestling team garnered nine medals in all. They discovered that a popular restaurant in the Castro district of San Francisco, known as *The Patio*, had offered all Gay Games medal winners a free meal. Monday night, the entire LA team sat down to eat dinner and emerged three hours later, their voracious appetites finally sated. With cupboards laid bare, *The Patio* retracted the offer later in the week.

Ray Geerlof and Jeff Greene are nearly inseparable. You get the feeling that these guys will be together for a long, long time. "We have a very good understanding of each other," Jeff concludes. "We each recognize that there are both 'adult' and 'child' elements in our personalities. It's okay to be silly and you don't always need to be grown up. There's a time and place for all of it." □

# Wrestling

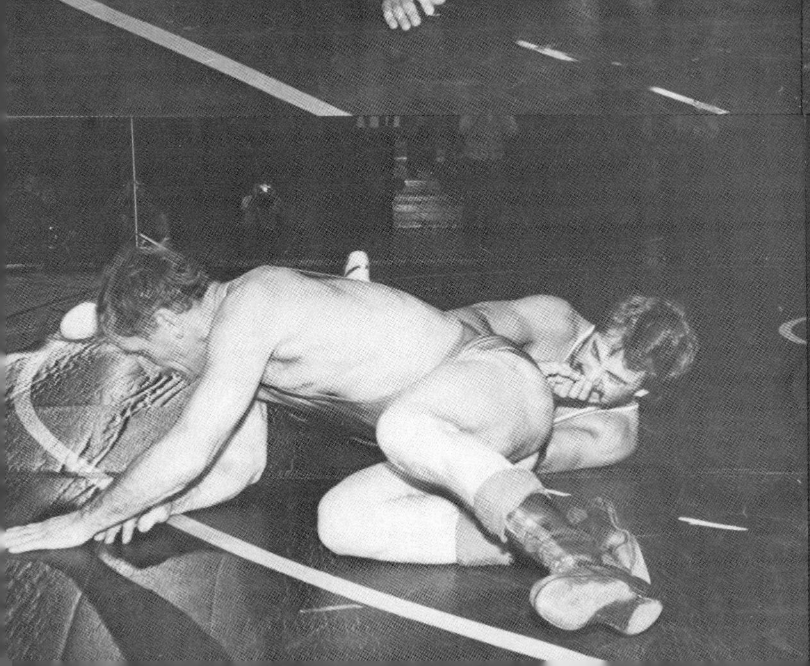

*"Hoooooooo honey!"*

# Carl Martin

WRESTLING ☐

SAN FRANCISCO, CALIFORNIA ☐

"I'm aggressive. I go for it from the second the whistle blows because I like the mental aspect of it. I like psyching somebody out. Totally. I won't be rude or unfriendly, but I'll have a look in my eye that says, 'I am after you and I'm going to do everything I can to beat you.'"

Carl Roger Martin leaned forward in his chair with a glint in his eye. "The second I was saying that, I could see myself wrestling *you*. The Games are only two days away and I'm almost crazy!"

Carl grew up in Lookout Mountain, Tennessee. His whole family was athletic, and his dad took it upon himself to push his first boy into many different sports. But Carl was not big enough for football, nor tall enough for basketball. In seventh grade his junior high school started a wrestling program and Carl found his place.

"In wrestling, you can be a champion no matter what size you are. You're not limited since you can on be top in your weight class. It only takes a split second to be there—if you make the right move, you can win. That's the beauty of it."

Carl excelled in the sport. In high school, at the Tennessee Military Academy, he placed first in the state championships two years in a row. "My coach told me that I had what they called balance. Balance is knowing exactly how far you can go with somebody in order to counter their moves."

He and a friend joined the Air Force and Carl ended up in a helicopter rescue and recovery team. The military sent him to school to acquire survival skills. He recalls "really getting into it. I was only seventeen, mind you, but I felt like GI Joe." He traveled throughout the Pacific and narrowly missed service in Vietnam.

While in the Air Force, Carl realized he was gay. But as a member of a flight crew who worked, slept and ate together, his secret remained untold. After six years Carl left the service with plans to move back to Tennessee. First, he stopped for a visit in San Francisco.

"After a week, I went home and came out to my family, cancelled my arrangements for school in Knoxville, packed up and moved out here. It's one of the best things I ever did. I feel like it's helped me grow in so many ways—not only spiritually, finding out who I am and being proud of it, but giving me the opportunity to meet people from different walks of life. Back in Tennessee I would have been very confined."

In 1982 his lover took him to the wrestling tournament at Gay Games I. Carl set his sights on winning a gold medal at the next Games in four years. He became Co-chair of wrestling and trained with the San Francisco wrestling club.

Two weeks before Gay Games II, Carl and a friend went to Kezar Pavilion to check out the facility. "The second I walked through the door, my heart skipped a beat. I looked down at the arena, then just ran down onto the floor. All of a sudden I could hear the noise of the people, and I could hear the announcement: 'Carl Martin, report to Mat Two.' That's what I've been waiting on now for three years."

Carl saw his dream come true in the wrestling tournament. His family flew out from Tennessee to watch him compete. While his lover Frank called out elapsed time from the edge of the mat, Carl swarmed over his competition and took the gold medal in the 163 pound class. I met one of his opponents from Los Angeles whose only comment on the match was: "I'd rather not talk about it."

I asked Carl how he felt about the sexual overtones of men's wrestling. "Sure, you might see someone who's hot, just like anywhere else," he replied. "But when the whistle blows, the *last* thing on your mind is sex. I don't care who you're wrestling or what he looks like. Maybe after the match, you go, '*Hooooooo, honey!*' But during those six minutes, being gay isn't part of it at all. I think that's really beautiful." ☐

# Special Moments

"Being gay is a constant evolution for the individual, and it's just as much an evolution for one's friends and family. Everyone needs time to grow and understand."
—Michael Hoche
Vancouver, BC, Canada

The Story of Gay Games II

## Procession of the Arts

The *Procession of the Arts* featured over twenty cultural events including dance, theater and art exhibits. (Left) "The Greatest of Ease" at Louise M. Davies Symphony Hall included a concert by the Lesbian and Gay Bands of America and several circus performers. (Lower left) "In Praise of Love and Sex" surveyed Japanese gay culture through the years. (Lower right) Jeffry Pike performs in "Conference Call," a series of modern dances.

All photos by Savage Photography.

# PROFILES

*"The power and force of sports, that total commitment of energy and abandon, is natural to me in the parts I'm given in the dance company. Then I take back to sports the calm subtlety and intelligence that is required to perform a movement and not make it be just superficial."*

# Jeffry Pike

☐ ATHLETE, DANCER

☐ BOSTON, MASSACHUSETTS

Jeffry Pike is an illustrator, dancer, athlete. In the year prior to Gay Games II, he helped pull together the Boston team, over a hundred strong. During the Games he performed with two friends during the Procession of the Arts. Jeffry Pike has a lot of energy.

He grew up in a sports-minded family. His mom was an active dancer. His dad coached baseball, track and soccer at the University of Connecticut, and later become head athletic trainer. Yet as a youngster, Jeffry preferred to stay inside and play.

He recalls his fondness for coloring, drawing, making clothes for his sister's dolls and watching old movies. He knew he was gay since the age of five. "One day, I remember it was winter, my father got me dressed up, put me outside and said, 'You're going to stay outside for an hour.' I remember crying and feeling lost . . . but somehow it connected."

With his natural abilities Jeff gradually found acceptance in both sports and musical theater in junior high and high school: "Performing was basically the only way I knew of to communicate with people... an escape because I couldn't face the adolescent part of being gay. In sports I was trying to stand up with my hands on my hips, giving attitude to people from the past who had made fun of me for being effeminate. I felt I had to prove something to them."

I interviewed Jeffry in the apartment he shares with friends in Somerville, Massachusetts. The introductions were formal and I began to wonder where my questions would lead. Jeffry told me that he had been thinking about this interview for several days, and he seemed shy and nervous. Finally the subject turned to dance, and Jeff's blue eyes sparkled with energy.

"I like sharing dance with people because it is a form of communication for me. It's a place where I get to reveal a lot of emotions.

"Over time, I have found that it's a way to bring pleasure to people. I've been fortunate to always see smiling faces as I walk off the stage. I think that keeps me going. I have something to share and I want to continue to share."

His idea for the dance performance during the Gay Games II cultural festival called on the talents of two friends who are also dancers. One lives in New York, the other in Washington, hence the title of their piece, "Conference Call."

They began by exchanging written correspondence; each artist outlined twenty-two moves. Next they met in rehearsal to decide how to interpret the choreography. Their performances involved solo, duet and trio work and was well received.

His participation in swimming and volleyball at Gay Games II offered different, less tangible rewards. He calls his team "another family." The sense of comaraderie and belonging helped motivate Jeff to organize other gay athletes in the Boston area.

In the swimming competition, he faced a tense moment when he was disqualified for a false start in his best event, the 100 yard breaststroke. Determined to face the pressure, Jeff came back the next day to win a bronze medal in the 50 yard breast. You've never seen anyone with a bigger smile.

"It's interesting how the dancing has helped my sports and sports have helped my dancing. They have really different qualities. The power and force of sports, that total commitment of energy and abandon, is natural to me in the parts I'm given in the dance company. Then I take back to sports the calm subtlety and intelligence that is required to perform a movement and not make it be just superficial."

ROY COE

Jeffry finds his energy diffused with so many different group activities. Yet they help to nourish his need for companionship and recognition, both on the playing field and on stage. He has worked hard to to overcome his tendency to be shy and withdrawn. With insight, he notes, "If I can say something physically, I am more comfortable with it." ☐

The Story of Gay Games II

118　　　　　　　　　　　　　　　　　　　　　　　　　　　　　　　　A Sense of Pride:

# ☐ Closing Ceremonies
### AUGUST 17, 1986

The Story of Gay Games II

(Below) *A signer for the deaf leans into a song along side vocalist Cindy Herron, and joyful athletes bid farewell to San Francisco.*

A Sense of Pride:

# MC / Closing Ceremonies

## Armistead Maupin

I am honored to be part of Gay Games II, because I regard this event as a potent force in the modern gay rights movement.

When we speak of gay pride, our pride is not really in being gay, but in telling the truth about it—telling it loudly and telling it often, because so many have lied about it for so very long. These lies have fostered an ignorance so enormous that preachers and presidents have stood idly by and clucked their tongues while thousands of good men were dying.

I would like to tell you that the death of these people has meant something. I would like to believe that their bravery has made us braver people, has opened our hearts and taught us to value the truth.

But then I hear gay people talking about the need for caution and discretion in these "repressive" times. "Sure," they say, "it's fine for *you* to be out of the closet, but I have to earn a living, and it would kill my parents if they ever found out. Besides, I give money to AIDS charities, I do my bit... I have my image to think about."

These people are not hiding from the problem, my friends, they *are* the problem.

They are every bit as homophobic as Jerry Falwell or Whizzer White or Lyndon LaRouche, and their self-loathing translates into misery and misunderstanding for honest lesbians and gay men everywhere.

For 2000 years we've remained invisible because of the hypocrites among us. Our triumphs and tragedies have been systematically erased from history by closeted people in the highest echelons—so much so that we are now forced to stage extravaganzas like this in order to justify our existence even to ourselves.

Sure, we are everywhere, but who among us really *believes* that? How *can* we believe it when the lies just keep on coming? Why do you think the U.S. Olympic Committee was so adamant in its opposition to the term "Gay Olympics"? Well, here's my theory: because they knew better than anyone that the term "Gay Olympics" is almost absurdly redundant.

There are locker rooms at the so-called "real" Olympics are so relentlessly homosexual that they look like a casting call for "Star Search."

I have a private fantasy I'd like to share with you. My fantasy is that Dr. Tom Waddell wins his battle with the U.S. Olympic Committee. The lawyers and judges relent, saying, "Go ahead, take it, the word is yours." And Tom replies:" Thank you very much, but you can keep your precious word—we've done just fine without it."

The operative word here is *gay*, not olympics. The operative purpose is *honesty*, not athleticism. A gold medal here doesn't mean a goddamn thing if you have to keep it out of sight when you get home.

MICK HICKS

122 A Sense of Pride:

## Shawn Kelly

For the past eight days we have witnessed the achievements of the most vibrant and talented members ever assembled from our community.

We have been inspired by their athletic excellence and by their personal triumphs. We have been moved and entertained by their dynamic artistry, and we have been overwhelmed by their enthusiasm and spirit felt here at our Ceremonies.

But in addition to those that we have seen, there is another group that deserves the same recognition, and the same praise and applause as our participating athletes and artists: I would now like to acknowledge the Gay Games II volunteers.

As Executive Director and the only employee of this organization, I have been amazed by the dedication of these men and women over the past two years. There were those who dropped their evening or weekend plans at a moment's notice to help with a desperate effort to send out a flood of mail, to put together one of our publications, to enter data on our computer, or to work on any one of a hundred other emergency projects.

And there were those who didn't limit their efforts to *small* projects, or to short-term needs, but who took on what amounted to full-time jobs. The committee and sports chair people who marched in behind me today have been the most outstanding examples of this type of "volunteer."

I know that they never *dreamed* of what they were getting into when they first took on these jobs. But let me tell you, if I had been able to pay for a staff, I couldn't have hired better leaders—or found better friends.

And, finally, I want to recognize those volunteers who do not live here in San Francisco, but who contributed nonetheless to these Games by organizing athletes in their own cities. They have been a major part of this endeavor and they, too, deserve your praise and applause.

In the end, what you have seen for the past eight days represents not just *my* idea of what Gay Games II should be, nor has it been the product of just a few people's vision. Rather, this festival has been the creation of the imagination, the talent and the dreams of *thousands* of people. Our "Triumph in '86" has first and foremost been *their* triumph.

There are those in our community who say that things have never been worse than they are today. And, truly, we face challenges and defeats that often reduce us to despair. But the accomplishments of Gay Games II demonstrate that we are *far* from defeated. Indeed, I believe we are stronger than ever before, and that Gay Games II is just a preview of even greater things to come.

As we communicate more with one another, as we work together on local, national and international projects, as we learn that our goals *are* within reach and that we *do* have the power to make them happen, we will find many such ways to show the world—and ourselves—why we exist as a community and why we love one another.

In an age when it is easy to curse the darkness, let the hard work of these thousands of Gay Games II volunteers shine forth as a candle of hope, and as a promise for our future.

Thank you for sharing this promise with us!

*The Board of Directors of San Francisco Arts & Athletics present Tom with a plaque that expresses their appreciation for his vision and leadership through the years. They honored him as 'Papa Games.' As Tom was introduced on stage, the athletes on the field began to chant: "Thank you Tom."*

124 A Sense of Pride:

## Dr. Tom Waddell

It has been a magnificent week. Athletes, you have made a *spectacle* of yourselves! And the whole world has noticed it.

Certainly we can all congratulate ourselves for achieving the goals of Gay Games II and the Procession of the Arts. Perhaps the most successful aspect of this week's activities was seen in the wonderful interactions between the women and the men athletes.

It was seen in the age-spread, with athletes ranging from seventeen to seventy. And the captain of one of the gay softball teams is straight, and black, and he felt like part of a family.

There were no national rivalries here, only cooperation and fun. For those of you who went to the circus concert of the Lesbian and Gay Bands of America, you saw one of the gay entertainment highlights of the decade.

This has been a week of remarkable achievement, and now Gay Games II and the Procession of the Arts have become historic reminders of who and what we really are, and what we've become. And what *have* we become?

We have talked for years about being teachers, and that is what we have become. We have something to teach a world that clearly seems to be going mad. We have taken responsibility for ourselves, particularly in the face of the AIDS crisis. We have set the standards for care and support. We will soon be teaching others.

With the activities of this past week we have demonstrated what tolerance, friendship and understanding can achieve. This world needs a lot more of these things, and we can give it.

Last week I suggested that we were the largest minority in the world. I want to modify that statement. In fact, I want to retract it. We are not a minority, we are an *alternative*. Everyone is welcome to our community. It is so simple: we like anyone who likes us.

We have many battles ahead of us before we achieve parity in our respective societies. There are people who fear our differences, who do not understand us. They will be educated through events such as those you have enjoyed this past week.

Please keep in mind also that we have many non-gay friends who support us. These Games would not have been possible without the cooperation of the Mayor, the Board of Supervisors, the Department of Parks and Recreation, and hundreds of others who make no judgments on us and who enjoy working with us.

It is a fact that a non-gay person who has gay friends is far less homophobic than someone who claims he doesn't know any gay people. Again, we need to put ourselves out there and educate. We are pretty nice people. We're worth knowing.

Last night, a friend of mine asked, 'What single thought would you like to leave the audience with today?' and this is it: We are the teachers of the eighties, and we are on the move!

*(Below, left) Helium balloons lie in wait for athletes. (Below, right) Athletes boogie on the field as Jennifer Holliday belts it out.*

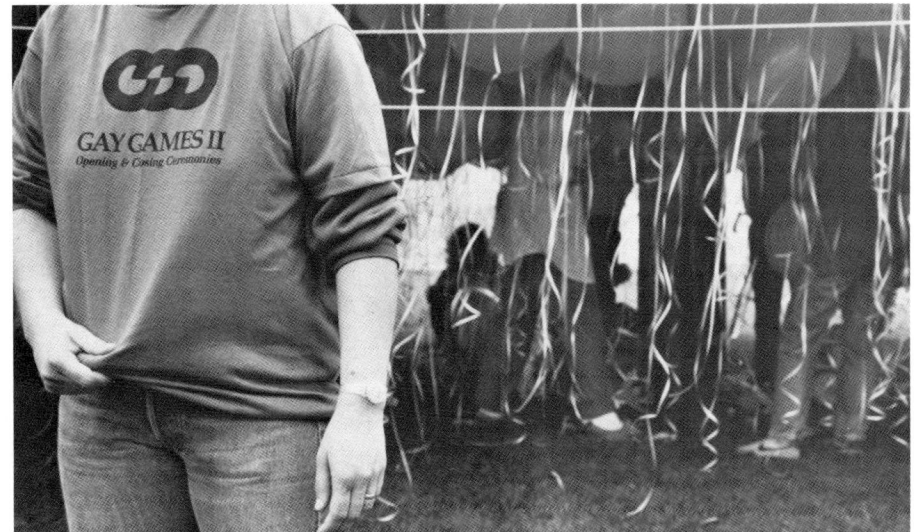

*The dream continues! Gay Games III was awarded to Vancouver, British Columbia for 1990. Richard Dopson, head of the Vancouver organizing committee, is shown accepting the Gay Games flag. For information on Gay Games III contact: M.V.A.A.A., 1170 Bute Street, Vancouver, B.C. V6E 1Z6, Canada.*